In Loving Memory of Emerson

In order to protect the identity of individuals involved in my story, their names have been changed.

Chapter 1

Hello, my name is Dan Koert and I am a heroin addict. I've been sober for six years. The reason I still refer to myself as a heroin addict, even though I'm clean, is because I will be a heroin addict till the day I die. Just because I am clean, doesn't mean that I'm suddenly cured. No, not at all. I have to battle this addiction every day. Some days are easier than others and at this point in my life, most days are pretty easy. Yet, when I find myself in a dark place, my demons come back and heroin seems to be the only answer. I know now how to fight these thoughts and to talk to people, but for a long-time heroin was my only coping mechanism. So, when times get tough, heroin seems to be the answer.

It took me a while to decide where to start this story. We could go all the way back to when I was a kid and go from there, but I decided that was boring. There was nothing significant that happened to me through the first fourteen years of my life. I was a typical kid who grew up in suburban Pennsylvania. I played sports and did well in school. I'm sure if you tried to tell my parents that I would become a heroin addict they would have never believed you. How can that happen to someone who was raised in a great home around a loving family that would do anything for them? Well, I'm here to tell you that.

This story begins with a boy and a girl on December 31, 2008. I had just turned fifteen and was in my freshmen year of high school. I went to a catholic school that was relatively small. We had about 130 students in my freshmen class. We all got along pretty well and I was on the football team, so I was pretty friendly with everyone. I wouldn't say I was popular, but I still got invited to most of the parties and had a group of close friends that I hung out with on the weekends.

Earlier on in the year, I had smoked weed for the first time. It became a weekend activity for my friends and me. It was really just something for us to do for fun. I wouldn't say that weed is a gateway drug at all. It didn't do much for me, but it was something for my group of friends to do together. I had tried drinking as well, but I really couldn't stomach the taste of it, so I guess that's why I chose to smoke weed instead of drinking.

Now that you're caught up, we can get back to December 31, 2008. Anna was having a New Year's Eve party for about thirty people from my class and I was invited. I wasn't really sure why I was invited because I never actually met Anna. She had come to our school in October. She had moved to the area and had to switch schools. The only reason I knew all of this was because I had noticed her on the day she visited our school.

I was sitting in my second period literature class, dozing off as always. Literature bored the shit out of me. I mean who wants to talk about Shakespeare at nine in the morning? My head was rested on my hand and my eyelids were getting heavy. Then, I heard the classroom door open, which caused my eyes to open back up.

In walked our guidance counselor and a girl I had never seen before. She was tall for a girl, about five-foot eight with long blonde hair and a curvy build. Considering the fact that she was only fourteen she looked like a fully developed woman. She was perfect in my eyes. In fact, I couldn't take my eyes off of her.

The guidance counselor introduced her, "Sorry to interrupt. I would like to introduce you all to Anna. She is visiting our school today to decide whether or not she would like to come here. I hope you all will be friendly to her and help her feel at home. Enjoy your day." As she spoke, Anna smiled and waved to the class.

Our teacher told her to take a seat in an empty desk that was five desks in front of mine. Anna walked over to the desk and took a seat. She put her backpack on the floor next to her and unzipped the top of it. She reached down and pulled out a folder and a pen. As she pulled these items out of her bag she looked back, right at me.

She had probably felt my eyes on her since she walked in the door, so of course that would cause her to look around. Or maybe she just wanted to see all the new people that could potentially be her classmates. She looked right at me though and smiled. I couldn't help but smile back. She turned back around to face the front of the classroom and try to pay attention to what the teacher was talking about.

Although we shared that brief moment, we never actually spoke to each other after that. She did end up coming to our school, but we didn't have any of the same classes together so we never ran into each other. That's why I was so confused on how I ended up with an invitation to the party. I had received the invitation through Facebook and it came from her. So obviously she knew who I was too. I tried to not think about it too much and just go and have a good time.

My friend and I were going to the party together. His mom was driving us because we lived closed to each other. Anna lived about forty-five minutes away. James's mom came to my house to pick me up and we were on our way to Anna's house. The three of us made small talk and talked about high school was going for the both of us.

James was one of my best friends. We had gone to grade school together and spent most of our free time together. We ended up going to different high schools though. He went to the local public school and I went to the catholic school. He became friends with my friends because of how close we were. That's why he was going with me tonight.

As we got close to Anna's, I started to get excited to be at the party and have some fun. James brought some weed with him in case we got the chance to get high. We were staying over another one of my friend's houses afterwards. We knew we were going to be able to smoke there, but we weren't sure if we would be able to smoke at the party.

We finally pulled into Anna's neighborhood. It was in a relatively new development. All of the houses looked exactly the same, but they were nice. We pulled into her driveway and Jake and I thanked his mom then got out of the car. We walked up to the door and I rang the doorbell.

The door opened almost instantly, it was Anna and another girl from my class, Laura. Anna greeted us, "Hey Dan! So glad you guys came." She hugged me as she said hello. "Who is your friend you brought with you?"

"This is Jake. He's one of my best friends. Hope you don't mind that he tagged along."

"Nice to meet you, Jake! It's no problem at all. I'm just so happy you could make it. Everyone is in the basement. Let me show you."

I couldn't help but think how weird it was how she greeted me. I literally had never spoken a word to her in my life. Yet, she greeted me like we were the oldest of friends. I was starting to think that she might have a crush on me too.

She led us to the basement and walked us down the stairs. The basement was unfinished, but fully furnished. It looked like we were the last people to arrive. Pretty much everyone else was already there. There were about forty people there. I knew everyone since it was all people from my high school. I guess you could say it was the more popular people.

Once Anna walked us down, we made our way around saying hello to everyone and bullshitting with people for a few minutes. Most of the people there already knew Jake from him coming to other events with me so we both fit right in.

I was sitting with a few of my friends on the couch making small talk when Anna came over and sat right next to me.

"Hey Dan, so happy we finally have a chance to talk!"

I was a little taken back by her being so up front with me. I wasn't used to girls seeking me out. "Yeah, me too. I don't think we ever actually had the pleasure of meeting."

"I know, that's why I invited you tonight. I wanted to formally meet you." She smiled at me with this playful look on her face. She was absolutely gorgeous. She was wearing a tight white dress tonight that hugged her body and made her blonde hair shine in the light.

"Well, I'm glad you invited me. I was kind of upset that we hadn't had the chance to meet yet. I have to tell you that you definitely caught my eye when you came to visit our school."

"Oh yeah?" She tilted her head a little bit and smiled at me. "You caught my eye too. That's why I invited you tonight, so we could get to know each other a little better."

"I figured you invited everyone here for that reason." I teased.

"You're different though, there's just something special about you."

I just smiled at her and she smiled back. I got lost in her sea blue eyes for a second. It was like her eyes held the answers to every question I ever had.

"You stay right here. I'll be right back." She got up and walked upstairs. I sat there thinking about what the hell just happened. Was that real? Did the girl I had a crush on from the moment I saw her have a crush on me too? I didn't have too much experience with girls at this point. I had kissed a girl, but hadn't done anything else. It was only because I hadn't had the opportunity yet. Maybe she would be the one.

I saw her come back down the stairs and she went off to one of the rooms in the back of the basement. She came back with two little bottles in her hand. I couldn't make out what they were. She came right back to the couch. Instead of sitting next to me, she sat right on my lap.

"I brought us something."

I looked at what was in her hand and it was two little shampoo bottles. "What the fuck is that? Are we going to wash our hair?" I laughed.

She unscrewed the cap and held the bottle up to my nose. "It's liquor! I had it in these little bottles so no one else knows."

"You think it's better that people think you're drinking shampoo?" I laughed.

"I guess you're right. I never thought about how dumb this was. So, do you want some?"

"I'm really not a big drinker."

She cut me off, "You're no fun."

"Woah, you didn't let me finish talking. I'm not a big drinker, but Jake has some bud on him if you want to smoke."

"Oh, you're more fun than I thought! Go grab him we can go smoke in the back room. There's a little window back there where we can blow the smoke. Do you care if Laura comes too?"

"That's fine. I'll go get him."

She hopped up off my lap to go find Laura and I got up to go get Jake. He was talking with a few of the guys. "Yo Jake, come here." I wanted to call him over so no one else could hear me tell him that we were going to smoke. "Anna said we can smoke in the back room. Let's go."

"Hell yeah man, I was getting bored. Glad she's cool with us smoking. What's up with you and her? I saw her all over you."

"I'm not really sure, but I'm pretty sure she likes me and I'm all about it. She's gorgeous."

"For sure dude."

We walked to the room in the back of the basement. Anna and Laura were already in there. It was pretty secluded. You couldn't see it from the part of the basement that everyone else was in so no one saw us all sneak off.

"Hey girls." I said.

"Hey!" They replied in unison with smiles on their faces.

Jake pulled out a bowl out of his pocket and an empty dip tin that he kept weed in. He grabbed a few buds and broke it up. He filled the bowl up with weed and sparked the lighter. He took a hit and passed it to me. I took a hit and passed it to Anna. We continued passing the bowl around for about ten minutes. We smoked two bowls and all decided that we were high. We headed back out to the party.

I went back to the couch and Anna followed me. We spent the next half hour getting to know each other a little better. Talking about her old school and how she moved here from Downingtown. After a little bit, she said, "Let me see your phone." I grabbed my phone out of my pocket and handed it to her. She took the phone and started doing something on it.

She handed me back the phone and said, "I want to talk to you more after tonight. I put my number in your phone."

I looked at my contact list and saw a new contact that said, "Anna <3." If there was any question about her being into me, that had answered it. "I want to keep talking to you too. You're really chill. You're not like the rest of the people at our school."

"What's wrong with the other people in our class?"

"Noting really, they just don't really smoke weed and kind of talk shit about me for smoking weed."

"Yeah, they are kind of lame. I guess that's the best way to put it. It seems like you and me get along really well though."

"Yes, it does. I'm glad you're not like them."

My friend Jacob walked over to me. "Dan, my dad's going to be here in about five minutes to pick us up. Just wanted to give you a heads up." A couple of my friends were all spending the night at his house. That's why Jake and I were going home with him.

"Sounds good."

I looked back at Anna and put my hand on her leg. "Well, it looks like I have to go soon. I really don't want to leave you."

"I know, but you can text me tonight!"

"Sounds like a plan to me." I smiled at her and she leaned in and gave me a hug. I hugged her for a little while and got up to go. We all left and got in Jacob's dad's car and headed back to their house for the night.

The rest of the night was spent smoking weed, watching movies, and most importantly texting with Anna. We stayed up late talking about nothing and everything. It was really nice to have someone that was so interested in me and my life. I hadn't ever had a real girlfriend before and was really into Anna already. She was the girl of my dreams.

I didn't know it at the time, but this night would change my life forever. It was one of those moments that I reflect on now that defined my entire life. We all have those moments that make us into the people we are. This night was the first major life defining moment for me. I sometimes wonder how my life would have went if Anna hadn't visited my class on her first day, or if she hadn't invited me to the party. I wouldn't change anything I've done in my life because everything that has happened to me has put me where I am today and I am exactly where I want to be. Yet, sometimes I like to fantasize about what my life would have been like had certain events not occurred.

I often wonder if I had never met Anna, would I still be a heroin addict? Would something else have led me to heroin or would I have chosen a different path? Is fate real? Was my fate to be a heroin addict or was it avoidable if I never went to that party? These are questions I like to ponder for fun sometimes. It just gives me a deeper perspective on life.

Chapter 2

Things progressed quickly with Anna and me. We would text all day and talk on the phone at night. We had been doing this since the night we met. We had an instant connection with each other and could not get enough of one another. We didn't see each other much at school so we decided to hang out the next Friday night. We planned to hang out at her house. This was just two weeks after we met.

Once we had planned to hang out, I was ecstatic. I could not wait for Friday to come and to spend more time with her. That week seemed to go by so slowly. It was like the clock was my worst enemy and it somehow managed to tick my slower.

Eventually, Friday finally came. School drug by, but eventually the final bell rang and I walked out to the bus. I hopped on the bus and put my headphones in for the ride home. I must have actually dozed off for a little bit and when I opened my eyes, I was at my stop.

I got off and headed to my house. When I got inside, I immediately hopped in the shower to get ready for the night. I made sure that I was all cleaned up for her and looked my best. My best consists of a nice pair of sweat pants and a nice hoodie. I'm a pretty simple guy.

My dad got home from work and I was out the door before he even came in.

"Woah there, I'm not even allowed to come inside first? He chuckled.

"Sorry Dad, I'm just excited. Can we go now?"

"Yeah bud, let me just run inside really quick and get changed."

I hopped in the car as he went inside. A few minutes later he came out and got in the car with me. We started the drive to her house. We didn't really speak too much. I've always been a little weird about talking about girls with my parents. I'm not sure what it was, but I just liked to keep to myself when it came to women. So, we talked about sports and school a little bit, but not about Anna. My dad bitched a little bit about how far away she lived, but when I told him that her parents were driving me home he lightened up.

As we got closer to her house, my stomach started to get butterflies. I had never experienced that because of a girl before. It was a strange sensation. I don't think I was nervous, just extremely excited. They got worse and worse the closer we got. By the time we pulled in her driveway, it felt like those damn butterflies were about to rip out of my stomach.

"Thanks dad! I'll see you later." I jumped out of the car before I even heard his reply. I walked up the walkway to the doorbell and rang the doorbell. At this point, I was sure that those butterflies were going to rip through my stomach. A few seconds passed and the door opened. It was Anna.

Immediately my butterflies were gone. All the anticipation that had led up to this moment and seeing her just alleviated all of my excitement. It wasn't that I was let down. It was just that this was what I had been waiting for. I was content. I was happy. "Hey babe." I said with a smile.

"I'm so happy to see you!" She exclaimed as she flung her arms around me and hugged me. "Come on let's go inside." She grabbed my hand and led me through the kitchen and into the living room, where she sat down on the couch and motioned for me to sit next to her. "My mom's upstairs doing stuff for work. She shouldn't bother us too much."

"Sounds good to me. I'm just happy to finally see you. So, do you want to watch a movie or something?"

"Yeah, let's see what's on." She grabbed the remote and started to flip through the channels. She came across the movie Click. "Do you like Adam Sandler?"

"Do I? Happy Gilmore is my all-time favorite movie. Let's watch it!"

She giggled and put it on. She set the remote down and snuggled up next to me. I put my arm around her and got comfortable. For the first time in a long time, I felt truly happy. I was completely content with life and was exactly where I wanted to be. I didn't want this moment to ever end. Life couldn't get any better than this moment in time. For once, I wasn't wishing to be somewhere else. I am always looking forward to what comes next and not living in the moment, except for now. I was living in the moment and I wanted to live in it forever.

We sat there quietly watching the movie. Enjoying each other's company. We had talked so much the last two weeks that I think we were both happy just sitting in each other's arms feeling each other's presence. We watched the entire movie without moving.

The ending credits started to roll and the song that was playing was, "You Get What You Give." She looked up at me with her perfect blue eyes. She was beautiful. I leaned down to kiss her and we had our first kiss. This was my first real kiss. I had little pecks before, but this was the real deal. We had our hands all over each other and our lips couldn't be broken apart. It's like our bodies were saying everything that we couldn't say with words.

We eventually moved off the couch and onto the floor. She was on top of me and our hands were all over each other. She slowly moved down my body and started to give me my first ever blowjob. I mean tonight was already my first real kiss so why not add first my blowjob to the list too.

She was working her magic on me and then I heard footsteps coming down the stairs. Really? This was when her mom finally decided to come down stairs? Anna must have heard it too because her head came off of me and quickly grabbed a blanket off the couch and threw it over us. We leaned back against the couch next to each other.

"Hey, you must be Dan!" Her mom had made her way down the stairs and was in the kitchen as she tried to have a conversation with me.

"Hello, Mrs. Wheeler. It's very nice to meet you." I said while my pants were completely down, under the blanket of course. What an awkward way to meet a girl's mother.

"It's my pleasure. Anna hasn't stopped talking about you since New Year's Eve. I don't mean to bother you guys. I just had to grab some paperwork."

"You're not bothering us." Anna replied as she looked at me and rolled her eyes. We were both completely aware of how much she had interrupted us.

"Well, I got what I needed. I'm heading back upstairs. We'll leave in about an hour to take you home."

"Whatever works for you Mrs. Wheeler. Thanks."

She walked back upstairs and Anna immediately whispered in my ear. "I want to have sex with you."

"Do you have a condom?"

"No, but we should do it anyway." She grinned devilishly at me.

"I really don't want to take a chance of getting you pregnant. I'll make sure I bring one next time. That way we'll have something to look forward to."

"Fine." She said that with so much attitude. It must not have bothered her too much though because she picked right back up where we left off before her mom came down. It didn't take too much longer for my first blowjob to be over.

Afterwards, we talked and made plans to hang out the following Friday. We decided that Friday nights were going to be our night. We would set that time aside to see each other every week. We both loved the sound of that.

"So, are we going to make this official?" She said.

"You mean like boyfriend and girlfriend?"

"Yeah dummy. I like you and you like me. I think at least."

"Uh yeah. That sounds great to me." I tried not to show it, but I was overwhelmed with the feeling of someone else liking me as much as I liked them. I had finally found what made my life whole and she was sitting right in front of me.

That night we became an official couple. We were now dating and could call each other boyfriend and girlfriend. I was on top of the world. They always say what comes up must come down. I never knew until now how great the highs were and I would soon find out how bad the lows are.

The next week drug on like usual. I was yearning for Friday to be here already. I was excited to see Anna and to lose my virginity to her. She had told me that she wasn't a virgin. She had lost her virginity to her last boyfriend. He was the only guy that she had slept with. That really didn't bother me though. I was just happy to be able to call her mine now and to soon lose mine to her.

That week we spent our usual amount of time on the phone with each other. Talking about school, our friends, our dreams, and everything in between. We shared everything with each other, holding nothing back. We had only known each other for a few weeks now, but it felt like we had known each other for years. Our conversations lasted for hours and ended with both of us not wanting to hang up the phone.

Finally, Friday arrived. My dad drove me to Anna's house yet again. As we got closer, those fucking butterflies started to come back. I could feel them fluttering around, getting more obnoxious the closer we got. I began to realize that this wasn't nerves, this was just how I got when I was excited to see her. I didn't know how to handle the anticipation so my body reacted with butterflies.

We eventually pulled into her driveway and I jumped out of the car. I hurriedly walked to the door and rang the doorbell. "Coming!" I heard Anna yell from inside. After a few moments, the door swung open and there she was. She was dressed in black leggings and tight tank top that showed off all of her best assets. I could not take my eyes off of her.

"I'm so glad you're here! I was getting so excited to see you!"

"I know babe, me too." I stepped inside and wrapped my arms around her. Holding her in my arms made everything right in the world. She was the solution to all my problems and worries.

"I told my mom that we were going to hang out in the basement tonight."

"Don't you think that makes it kind of obvious?" I smirked.

"What do you mean?" She teased as she turned her back to me. Then she turned her head back to look at me with a devilish look in her eyes. "Follow me!" She reached back and grabbed my hand and led me downstairs.

We walked down the stairs and made our way for the couch where we spent our first night together. We sat down next to each other and wasted no time. I moved closer to her and put my hands on her hips. Our heads drew closer and our lips met. Our hands explored each other's bodies as our tongues twirled.

I started to take her clothes off slowly, piece by piece. Admiring her perfect body as each piece of clothing came off. After a few more minutes she was completely naked, as was I. I thought she was perfect before, but now I knew she was perfect. Staring at her bare body in the light, I saw how flawless she truly was. I wanted her so badly. In fact, I needed her.

She grabbed some blankets off the couch and threw them down on the floor. She laid back on top of them and motioned with her finger for me to come with her. I climbed down on top of her and began kissing her again.

I'm going to spare you guys the graphic content. I think you know what happens next. This time, I came prepared with protection and was ready to lose my virginity to her. That was exactly what happened. We've all had our first experiences with sex, so there's no need to elaborate on the details. The only strange part about it was she cried from pain during some of it. She had told me she wasn't a virgin so I was sort of confused on why it hurt so much for her. It made me think that maybe she had lied about not being a virgin. That maybe that was her first time. I really didn't care one way or the other. I just would have preferred that she was honest with me.

After we finished, I climbed off of her. "That was amazing." I told her as she sat back on the couch and I began to put my clothes back on."

"Sorry for all the crying, it's been a while since I've had sex, so it hurt a little bit. The more we have sex, the less it'll hurt. I just have to get used to it again."

"It was a little weird at first, but I understand. I'm not opposed to having more sex." I grinned.

I finished putting my clothes back on and sat back on the couch. I watched her as she stood up and began putting her clothes back on. She was perfect in every form of the word. I never wanted to lose this girl. It wasn't just about her looks though. Our personalities fit perfect with each other. It was like I had found the person I was supposed to be with.

She finished getting dressed and sat back on the couch with me. She laid her head down in my lap and she got comfortable. I put my hand on her hip and we just sat there like that for a few minutes, thinking about what had just transpired.

"Dan, I want to tell you something."

"You know you can tell me anything."

"Well, I know we haven't known each other for very long, but I love you."

I was completely taken back by that. I hadn't really thought about it. I never knew what love was. Sure, my parents loved me and my friends loved me, but I didn't know what love was in a romantic relationship. I thought that it actually described perfectly how I felt about her. It just hadn't clicked for me yet. "I love you too."

She smiled at me with those deep blue eyes, "I wasn't sure how you were going to react to that. I know it seems quick, but I just can't help how I feel."

"I know exactly what you mean. Time doesn't really mean anything though. Sometimes things happen quickly and I think you and I have grown extremely close in a short period of time."

"I'm so happy that we finally had the chance to meet and get to know each other. I wasn't sure if you were going to like me or not."

"Isn't that what life's all about? Taking chances, rolling the dice and seeing how they land?"

"You're right. I'm glad I took a chance and invited you to my party. I have to be honest, I had the party just so you and me could meet."

"Really? You did all that just for me?"

"Yeah, Laura and I were talking about how I could get a chance to talk to you and we decided that having a party and inviting you was the best way to do it." She blushed as she said that.

"That's awesome!" I couldn't help smiling like an idiot. I couldn't believe she did all that just to have the opportunity to talk to me. "Well, I'm glad you did all that work just so you could meet me."

"Me too."

We spent the rest of the night on that couch talking. Just enjoying the company of each other. The night seemed to fly by. Before we knew it, we heard the basement door open and Anna's mom yell down. "Guys, it's time to take Dan home! Let's get ready to go."

"Okay mom, we will be up in a minute."

We spent that last minute holding each other not wanting to let go. Eventually, we decided that it was time to head upstairs and start the trip back to my house.

That night I hold onto as a fond memory. Writing about it brings me back to that moment and how amazing it was to feel love for the first time from another person. That night will always be a cherished memory. I think the reason I hold it so closely is because it was our last night together with no bad memories. Everything was good and it seemed like her and I were going to be together forever. It turns out I didn't realize how short forever really was.

Chapter 3

Life was good. Life was really good. I had the girl of my dreams and that was all that I cared about. Everything I did revolved around her. My time was either spent talking to her or wishing I was talking to her. I couldn't get enough of her. She had become the strongest drug I ever took and I was addicted.

Life was not going to be good for much longer though. The best way to describe my relationship with Anna was by comparing it to a roller coaster. So far, we had just fastened our seat belt and began the slow climb up to the top. We were about to reach the peak though and begin the quick decent into madness. There would be twists and turns, highs and lows, times that life got flipped completely upside down and times that I wasn't sure if I would survive the ride and times that I just wanted the ride to end.

The next couple weeks went by as usual. We hung out on Fridays and spent the rest of the week talking to each other. There wasn't a moment that passed without us thinking about each other. Our worlds had become entwined and we couldn't separate them. We didn't want to separate them either. We began to live our lives as if we were one in the same.

The next Friday rolled around and Anna and I were in her living room. We were both completely naked. With her mom, just up the stairs in her room, doing whatever the hell she did while we had the house to ourselves basically. We were having sex yet again. It had become a part of our Friday routine.

We finished and I was startled when I realized the condom wasn't on me anymore. "What the fuck? What happened to the condom?"

"What do you mean what happened to the condom?"

"Well, it's not on me and I don't know where the hell it went."

"You better find it and it better not be inside me. Did you finish?"

"Yeah I finished." I started looking around us. Looking underneath the couch and between the couch cushions. Not understanding what had happened to that stupid piece of rubber.

"I better not be pregnant."

"Yeah, I definitely hope not. I don't want a kid." I looked everywhere, but couldn't find it. There was only one possibility left. "I think its inside you."

"What the fuck!" She jumped up off the couch and went to the bathroom. She was in there for what seemed like forever. I put my clothes back on while I waited for her and set her clothes neatly on the couch for her. I was thinking about all the possibilities. Mainly, if she was pregnant. What the fuck would we do?

The bathroom door opened and Anna came out. I could see tears streaming down her face. She was sobbing like a child who had their favorite toy taken away. She came over to the couch and started getting dressed.

"Well, was it in you?"

"Yeah, now I'm probably pregnant. I can't have a baby. I can't believe that just happened. How did you not know that it came off? Doesn't it feel different with it off? Why did this have to happen?"

"Easy, calm down babe."

"No, I can't be calm when I might be pregnant."

"We'll figure this out."

She had finished putting her clothes on and walked into the kitchen. I decided to follow her in. I knew something was wrong and wanted to comfort her, but I didn't know how to. So, I figured being close to her was all that I could do. I watched as she reached up into one of the cabinets and pulled out a bottle of pills. She twisted the cap off and poured some pills into her hand. She tilted her head back and put the handful of pills in her mouth. Then, she went over to her parent's liquor cabinet and grabbed a bottle of vodka. She took a long drink from the bottle. She drank like she was dying of thirst and hadn't had liquid in three days.

I watched not knowing what the fuck was going on. What the fuck was she doing? Something was wrong, very wrong. Whatever just happened was a side of Anna I had never seen before. What was she doing? I knew that she could be pregnant, but that's not the end of the world. There are ways of taking care of that. For me, nothing was that bad as long as I had Anna by my side. I knew that we would get through this together. She apparently thought different. She was going to get through this with a bottle of liquor.

I was no longer her solution. She had problems that I couldn't solve. The solution for her was at the bottom of a bottle and that hurt. I still couldn't wrap my head around what just happened, but it killed me that I wasn't able to help her anymore. She had found her solution from something else.

Tears began to well up in my eyes and I could feel the first tear run down my cheek. Anna was now sitting in front of the liquor cabinet crying. Her head was between her knees. I walked over to her and grabbed her hand. I guided her back to the couch like she had guided me so many times. She had been the leader for so long that now it was my turn to lead her.

We sat down on the couch. I grabbed her and held her tighter than I ever had before. The tears were now trickling down my face, but I didn't make any sounds. I didn't want her to know that I was crying. I couldn't be weak when she needed me to be strong. I needed to be there for her in her moment of weakness.

We sat there in silence, except for her muffled sobs. There were no words that needed to be said. There was no way of telling her that things would be okay. She didn't believe that. It was like her world had come crashing down around her.

That's how the rest of the night was spent. Anna crying, with me holding her trying to just be the comfort that she needed. Eventually, her sobbing subsided. I guess the pills and alcohol were finally kicking in. She was being comforted by the drugs and they made the pain hurt a little less. She was numbed by the effects and was able to forget about what had just happened.

The time had come for me to go home. We both got in her mom's car. Anna sat up front and I sat behind her in the backseat. The ride home was quiet, but she had reached back behind her so that I could hold her hand the whole way home. That comforted me that she still wanted to feel my touch, still feel that I was there for her.

I got home and went straight to bed. I was exhausted from the events that had taken place. I didn't want to talk to anyone or be disturbed so I put my phone on silent. Before I put it down, I sent Anna a text. "I love you no matter what, goodnight." Then I put my phone down and quickly drifted off to sleep.

The next morning, I woke up and looked at phone immediately. I had twelve missed calls from Anna. I instantly called her back. The phone rang once and she answered.

"Hello?" Her voice sounded very distant like she was talking from miles away, but I could hear her perfectly fine.

"What's going on? I had twelve missed calls from you."

"I'm in the hospital."

"What? What happened? Are you okay?"

"I'm going to be okay. They had to pump my stomach."

It clicked, holy shit, they had to pump her stomach from all the pills and alcohol she drank the night before. I don't know why I didn't realize how dangerous what she did was. My mind must have been clouded from all the emotion of what was going on that I couldn't see that she had tried to kill herself last night. The pills and alcohol wasn't to make her feel better. It was to end it all. She didn't want to live anymore. The possibility of having a baby at fifteen was too much for her to handle. I responded, "Holy shit, who took you to the hospital?"

"My mom."

"How did she find out that you needed to go?"

"She heard me fall in my room and came in to check on me. I wasn't responding to her so she got me in the car and took me here."

"I'm so sorry babe."

"It's okay, I'm going to be okay. They just came in to do a few more tests on me so I have to go. I'll call you later."

"Okay, I love you."

"I love you too."

That fucked me up. I had never seen that side of Anna before. Sure, we smoked weed together, but she never said anything to me about pills. I couldn't believe that she had actually tried to kill herself and that I literally just watched. It never clicked last night that she was trying to hurt herself. I couldn't believe that I was so naïve. How could I not have realized what happened? I think I was just so emotionally fucked up that I was completely blinded. I had seen a side of her that she hadn't shown before. I was left with no solutions, apparently my mind didn't even work to tell me what had just happened.

That was it. Her demons finally came out to play. They waved their gnarly little claws at me and showed me that they existed. Anna was far from perfect. Suicide had become her only solution. I didn't know that she was hurting so badly on the inside. She always seemed so happy-go-lucky. Her demons had disguised themselves so well.

That night was the first time I was introduced to her demons. I didn't know it yet, but they would become more prevalent very shortly. Her demons would come out to play again very soon. They would take control of her and introduce themselves to my demons. It would turn out that our demons got a long very well together. In fact, we would share some of the same demons.

After that, we pretended like it never happened. We pretended like there was no chance that Anna was pregnant and that she had never tried to kill herself. I didn't know how to deal with these facts and neither did she so we just brushed them under the rug. Neither of us wanted to believe that either of those things had happened. So, we tried to go back to how things were before that night.

We continued our routine of hanging out on Friday. I got to her house and her mom answered the door. "Hey Dan, come on in. Anna's upstairs in the shower. Just make yourself at home."

I walked into the house and made my way to the living room. I sat down on the couch and turned the television on. I began flipping through the channels attempting to find something to watch. I eventually decided to just put on some random movie I had never seen before.

I could hear the shower running upstairs. I anxiously waited for Anna to finish up and come down. I missed her and just wanted to have her in my arms. I wanted to hold her and tell her that everything was going to be alright, even if that was a lie. I didn't know if everything was going to alright after what happened. That night had changed everything.

The shower stopped. After a few minutes, I heard the bathroom door open and footsteps coming down the stairs. Anna came around the corner. I looked up at her. She looked different. She no longer had that glow about her. Her blonde hair didn't shine like it used to. Her face sported an attempted smile, but it wasn't the smile I fell in love with. She looked like she had been through a battle and lost.

"Hey babe." She spoke very softly. She sat down next to me and put her legs over mine.

"Are you okay? You look like you're sick."

"I have something I need to tell you." She whispered in my ear. She proceeded to lightly grab my hand and run it along the crook of her arm. I could feel little bumps. I had no idea what they were.

"What are those?"

"Those are track marks."

"What the hell is that?"

"It's from shooting heroin. There the marks that get left behind from where I put the needle in."

What did she just tell me? Did she really just say that she's a heroin user? Who was this girl sitting next to me? This was not the person I fell in love with. Everything I thought I knew about her was gone and replaced by what seemed like someone else. I couldn't believe what I had just heard. "Why didn't you tell me about this before?" I stammered.

"I haven't done it in a long time. My friends and I did a lot of drugs. It's part of the reason I switched schools. My parents thought it would be good for me to get away from my old friends. I didn't tell you because I thought this part of my life was behind me."

I didn't know what to say. I felt tears welling up in my eyes again. I tried to wipe them back. I was fighting with everything in me to not show how much I was hurting. I lost the fight, tears started streaming down my face. She reached up and wiped them away for me.

"I'm sorry." She said. "I need you to know I love you. Sometimes the pain just gets too great for me and this is the only answer."

I had nothing to say. I was attempting to comprehend all of the events that had taken place in the last week. First, Anna tried to kill herself and now I find out that she's a heroin user. I had never dealt with anything like this before. Heroin used to just be some word that we learned about in school that only degenerates use. It was just a word. Now that word had meaning.

It turns out that not just degenerates do heroin, people you love do heroin. It creeps into your home and destroys it from the inside out.

Heroin doesn't discriminate. It found its way into a girl's life who came from a rather wealthy family who lived in a good area.

Heroin now had meaning for me. It meant that the girl I thought I knew and loved was doing it. She had found her escape in a needle. She had somehow managed to get away from it for a little while, but life happened and she turned back to the only answer she knew, heroin.

This was my first taste of heroin, no I didn't try it. You don't have to try heroin to taste it. You get tastes of it from other people. You see what it does to them and it leaves its effect on you. Heroin had made its way into my life.

I finally put together some words, "How did this happen?"

"I got into drugs because most of my friends were doing them. They either took pills from their parents or just started buying and selling them. Most of my friends are kind of rich and their parents would give them a good bit of money. So, we always had money and our parents weren't around much, so we ended up doing drugs. It all started with OxyContin. Eventually, that turned into heroin."

"Why did you ever try heroin? I've always heard how addictive it was. I would never do that shit."

"We were already doing Oxys so it didn't seem that bad. We had heard that heroin was even better so we figured we would give it a try. It turns out, it was even better. I loved it from the first time I did it. I couldn't get enough."

"How did you afford all that shit? I know it's not cheap."

"My friends started selling Oxys and they were making good money. Since I hung out with them, they were just giving me stuff for free. They weren't too worried about money."

"That's crazy. I can't believe you got caught up in that shit."

"I know. I'm sorry you had to find out like this. I thought I was done with it forever." She paused for a second. "I love you."

"It's okay, we'll get through this. I love you too."

The rollercoaster had taken another abrupt turn. One that I never saw coming. I never could have imagined that this perfect girl would have so many flaws. This was my first glimpse of life. Until now, I had been a sheltered kid who was rather naïve to all the demons in the world. I never thought that heroin would become a part of my life, especially through the love of my life.

I had never known pain like this until now. Sure, physical pain was one thing. I had broken my collar bone before. I knew what that felt like, but I never experienced emotional pain like this. I felt empty, like there was something missing from me. Anna's demons had worn off on me and stolen a piece of me that I could never get back.

Chapter 4

The rollercoaster ride was far from over. Many things had been thrown at me over the last week and I was not handling it well. My mental state was deteriorating and I was becoming withdrawn from everyone. I would come home from school and go to straight to my room for the rest of the night. Spending my time listening to music while talking to Anna off and on.

She was the only connection I was hanging onto in hopes that this was just a really bad dream that I would soon wake up from. I would wake up and everything would go back to how it was before the night she tried to kill herself. I just wanted everything to go back to the way it used to be. A time before I found out that monsters are real. That they live inside of all of us and that it just takes a small prod to wake them up.

I could tell that Anna was using more and more. Our conversations became briefer and she became more distant. Even the time we did spend on the phone, you could tell her mind was elsewhere, although it was probably just clouded by the heroin. She wasn't herself and it was killing me. I just wanted the girl I loved back. I wanted to take the pain away for her, but I couldn't. Heroin could though.

The worst part about all of it was that I didn't want to tell anyone that Anna was a heroin addict. She didn't ask me to keep it a secret, but I felt the need to. I didn't want everyone at school to judge her based on a few poor decisions she made, so I kept it to myself. That means I had to deal with it on my own, which was not easy. I mean, how the fuck is a fifteen-year-old supposed to cope with their loved one shooting heroin? I still don't know the answer to that question.

I had become very emotionally unstable and things with Anna had gotten worse. She decided that we shouldn't be together anymore. This conversation happened over the phone. I told her that I didn't want anyone else and only wanted her. I wanted to help her get through what was going on in her life and be a part of her life. She simply said that she couldn't do it anymore. I asked if we could remain friends and she agreed.

Our "friendship" continued just like our relationship. We spoke just as often as we used to. We never lost that connection. The only difference was we stopped hanging out on our night, Friday. The first Friday night I spent without her was lonely. It killed me not being with her. All I wanted was to hold her in my arms and have that feeling of comfort that she provided to me. I was now empty inside.

Anna had found her new solution, heroin. She was able to cope with life and its circumstances by using a substance. She had gained a means of dealing with the seemingly insurmountable. Me on the other hand, had lost my solution. Anna was my solution to my problems. I no longer felt whole. I felt like a piece of me was missing and nothing filled it. Smoking weed didn't even help. It just made me even more depressed.

My life was spiraling down. Without Anna, I didn't know what to do. My life felt meaningless. I didn't want to live in a world that didn't have Anna in it.

Another Friday rolled around and I was on my way to school. I texted Jake, "Dude, I don't want to do this anymore. I'm done."

"Did she really fuck you up that bad?"

"Yeah man, like I don't even want to be alive anymore."

"Don't say that type of shit dude, it's not funny."

"I'm serious. I think I want to kill myself."

"You can't. That's not the answer to this shit."

"I'm doing it tonight."

"Can you please come over my house first? I want to see you one last time."

"Yeah, I can do that."

I'm not sure why I agreed to go over his house first. Maybe it was my last call for help. Maybe he would be able to tell me something that would stop me from doing it. I don't know though because my mind was made up and once I decide on something, I'm pretty stubborn. I was done with life and wanted to find out what the next life held in store for me. I knew it couldn't be worse than this.

After school, I went over to Jake's house. I walked in through the door to his basement where I knew he'd be. He was sitting there on the computer doing something. I really didn't care what he was doing. "So, I'm here."

"Thanks for coming over dude."

"I figured I'd at least come say goodbye."

"So, you seriously want to do this?"

"Yeah, I can't handle life anymore. Anna was the only thing I ever wanted and I can't have her. So, this is it I guess."

"How are you going to do it?"

"Do what?"

"Kill yourself."

"Um, I don't know. I honestly didn't even think about it."

"You're not going to do it then."

"Is that a challenge?"

"No, not at all. If you were serious about it you would have done it already. You wouldn't have told me. I think you just reached out to me because you needed help."

"Damn, I didn't even think about that. I just really feel like I want to die, but I guess I actually don't want to die."

"Yeah, shit sucks sometimes man. How about you spend the night here and we'll just kick it and chill the fuck out."

"That sounds good to me. I could use some time to just chill."

"I've got some good ass weed too. We can get high and play some video games. We can talk about her too if you want."

"Sounds good to me. I think I would actually prefer not talking about her. I just want to try to forget about her for the night."

"That works for me."

I hopped on his other computer and went on Facebook and played some games. We just sat there in silence, but in the company of each other. It was nice to have a friend to spend some time with. I had been spending so much time with Anna that my friends had kind of fell by the wayside. I still saw them on Saturdays, but I used to spend the whole weekend with them. I missed them and I hope they missed me too. I was happy to be with them on a Friday night.

We spent the rest of the night smoking weed and just hanging out. Anna wasn't spoken of and I did my best to push her out of my mind. It worked for the most part. She would still pop in occasionally, but I would just push her back out. I had a really good night. The first good night I had had in a long time.

The next day, Jake and I decided to go see some of our other friends. His mom took us to their house. Once we got there we decided to head to a church parking lot that was nearby. We hung out here quite often. We would just chill, throw a football around or sometimes a Frisbee.

When we got there, there were a few other guys there already. They weren't my friends, but we did all know each other. We began talking with them and they started telling us about these pills they had tried for the first time. They were cough medicine pills that you could buy at the store, but the active ingredient in them fucks you up. They said it was the most fucked up they had ever been.

Jake and I looked at each other as they were talking. We didn't say anything, but we knew that we were going to go get some after this and try them tonight. Anna had been escaping through drug use, so why shouldn't I? I wanted to feel the same sense of numbness that she was. I didn't want to do heroin, but these pills sounded like a great alternative.

We spent the rest of the afternoon hanging out at the parking lot. Enjoying the day with our friends. We talked and laughed and it felt good to finally feel like a part of the group again. I had been pulled away because of Anna, but now I was back. I felt at home.

Just before Jake's mom came back to pick us up, we walked over to the CVS. It was right across the street from the parking lot we were at. We were going there so we could buy the pills. As we walked, Jake said, "You know they are going to card us when we try to buy them?"

"Shit, really?"

"Yeah, so I figured I would just steal them."

"I'm trying to get fucked up tonight so that sounds awesome to me."

"I'll go in and grab them. I'll buy something else so it's not obvious that I'm stealing. Just wait out here for me. I'll be right back."

Jake walked inside. I stood off to the side of the store and waited for him. I hoped that he wouldn't get caught because I was really excited to try a new drug tonight. I had never done anything besides weed and these pills sounded like they were going to make me feel exactly how I wanted to.

A few minutes later, Jake walked out. We started walking back to my friend's house where his mom was going to pick us up. "So, how'd it go?" I asked.

"Shhhhh." He reached in his sweatshirt pocket and just flashed me the corner of a package.

I knew that meant he had gotten them and that we were going to be getting high tonight.

We made it back to his house and went straight into his basement. Jake walked over to his desk and grabbed the package of pills out of his pocket and placed the on the desk. He looked over at me. "You ready?"

"You know it."

He ripped open the package and emptied the contents on to the desk. There were two silver trays with eight little red pills in each. They looked like skittles. In fact, that's the name we gave them. "So, Mikey said that they split a pack. So, that means we each get a tray." He handed me one of the little trays filled with skittles. I eagerly grabbed them from him and walked over to the other desk and sat down.

I could hear that Jake had started popping the pills out of the container and I started to do the same. I poked all eight pills out of the tray and placed them in a little pile on the desk. I turned around and said, "Let's do this shit." Without even a response, Jake threw all eight pills in his mouth and swallowed them with a drink of water.

I picked the pills up off the desk and held them in my hand for a minute. Anna used to be the answer to all my problems, but now she had become part of the problem. Maybe these pills would be my new solution. I tilted my head back and put the pills on my tongue. I grabbed my water and took a swig. The pills were relatively small so, they went down pretty easy.

Now it was time to wait. Mikey had told us that it took about an hour for the pills to kick in. That meant we had some time to kill before we started feeling it. Jake put some music on and we both found things to do on the computer while we waited. It was only a matter of time before they kicked in.

My mind was completely off of Anna now. I wasn't high yet, but just knowing that I was going to be numb soon made me forget about her. My thoughts now were just on how these pills were going to make me feel. My hopes were that they would make me numb and completely forget about Anna for the night.

There was no regret or fear about taking the pills. I mean, we got them at a drug store. They are available for anyone to buy so they can't be that dangerous. Just a little harmless fun for a night. At least I wasn't doing heroin, right?

After about forty-five minutes, I started to feel a little different. My body felt heavy, but I couldn't really feel anything. Not physically, emotionally. I was completely numbed. All my worries were gone, my pain was gone, and most importantly Anna was gone. I guess I shouldn't say she was gone since she did cross my mind. Yet, when she did cross my mind, I didn't care. She no longer had a stranglehold on my life. For the first time, in a long time, I was free.

I started smiling as the drugs took control over me. Over the next couple of minutes, I felt the drugs kicking in even harder. I stood up to see how they affected my motor skills, and it turns out walking while on these was a little strange. The ground felt like Jell-O. When I took a step, it felt like my foot would sink into the ground a little bit. It was a strange feeling but, I was enjoying it.

"Yo dude, you got to try walking. The ground feels like Jell-O!" Jake got up and started to walk around the basement. He stumbled a few times, but he started to figure out how to walk with the ground jiggling underneath him.

"This shit's crazy! I can't believe we never did this before."

"Dude, I'm loving this. You got any cigs or weed?"

"You know I always have both."

"Let's go chill outside and smoke."

Jake grabbed his tin of weed, a bowl, and a pack of cigarettes from a drawer in the desk. He walked out of the door and I followed him. We headed over to our usual spot. A hammock with a few chairs placed just outside of the basement. We spent many nights out here smoking and hanging out.

He took a seat on one of the chairs and I took a seat on the hammock. Well, I tried to take a seat. I more or less fell into the hammock. I laid back and looked up at the stars and got lost in them for who knows how long. I was staring into the deep abyss of space and it felt like it was staring back at me. I came back around when I heard Jake say, "Take the bowl man." I grabbed the bowl from him and sparked the lighter. I inhaled deeply as the weed filled my lungs.

It felt different then every other time I had smoked weed. I'm guessing it was because I had already taken drugs. Just the one hit of weed intensified my high. The feeling of numbness became even greater and my mind was elsewhere. I don't know where it was at, but it was exactly where I wanted it.

"I don't need any more of that. I'm fucking gone."

Jake laughed, "Me too dude. Those pills got me fucked up. You want a cig?"

"Yeah, I'll take one."

I took a cigarette from him and lit it. I took a drag and watched the cherry light up as I inhaled. The colors looked extremely cool. The drugs were having an effect on my vision. I wasn't hallucinating, but the colors and how things moved were kind of slowed down. I was getting lost in my own mind. Everything seemed new to me. It was like I was given a different perspective on life and I was really enjoying it.

The rest of the night was spent outside just hanging out and enjoying our new-found escape. We talked some, but mostly we just basked in the high we were both experiencing. We eventually decided to head inside and try to get some sleep. I was still high as a kite, but decided sleep was probably a good idea. I drifted off pretty quickly.

The next morning, I felt a little shitty. Most likely from coming down off the pills. That wasn't the bad part though. The bad part was that all my feelings and emotions were back. Anna was on my mind again and I fucking missed her. I wanted her back in my arms. All the events that happened with her the last few weeks came flooding back into my mind. All the pain had returned.

I had found a temporary solution to my problems in the pills. They allowed me to escape from reality for a few hours, but it was a rude awakening having to feel everything again. I really wanted to escape again and go back to how I felt or I guess I should say, how I didn't feel last night. I knew I couldn't do more today, but I really wanted to.

That night was the first time that I danced with my demons. We locked hands and did the most beautiful ballroom dance that anyone had ever seen. My demons looked beautiful that night as I spun them around the dance floor. That would be the first dance we had in our epic ballroom saga. It would be a dance that lasted for the next four years. After that, my demons would offer me a dance for the rest of my life and I would have to do my best to decline.

Those pills I took turned out to contain an active ingredient called dextromethorphan, DXM for short. It turns out that they were dissociatives. That explained why I felt so numb. Basically, they are a type of psychedelic drug. That's why colors were moving around and my mind seemed to wander.

That night began my relationship with DXM. It turned into my escape that I utilized way too often. It was my first serious drug and I loved it. It did things for me that weed never could. It became my coping mechanism, my escape and above all my best friend. It provided a solution to me that nothing else could. That piece of me that Anna had taken could be filled with DXM. It made me whole again.

Chapter 5

Anna and I didn't talk at the all that weekend. She did her own thing and so did I. My own thing consisted of me trying a new drug and falling in love with it. I didn't tell Anna what I did and had no intention of telling her anytime soon. It was the first secret I was keeping from her.

That Monday morning, I was at my locker and I glanced over and saw Anna walking up to me. She looked beautiful again. It seemed like she hadn't been doing heroin. I don't think anyone else ever noticed the difference in her, but I definitely did. I could look at her and see if she was on or not. She definitely was not on. Her smile was back and that aura that she carried around her was back as well. The girl I loved had found her way back to me.

She walked up to me. I was kneeling in front of my locker. She knelt down beside me. "So, I've been thinking. I don't think I want to be your friend anymore." She paused.

My heart fucking sank. Was this really going to be the end of us? Was she really calling it quits? She finally had her luster back and she was going to leave me for good.

"I want to be your girlfriend." She smiled at me with that smile that felt like home.

"I fucking love you." I smiled back and put my arms around her. "I missed you."

"I missed you too."

"I'm sorry to cut this short, but I got to get to class. The bells about to ring. I'll talk to you later."

I grabbed my books and headed off to class. Everything was right in the world once again. I had my girl back and everything was going to be okay. Hopefully, last weekend was just a one-time thing and there would be no more pills in my future. Also, hopefully there was no more heroin in Anna's future.

This rollercoaster of my freshmen year had just begun. I thought that it had finally came to an end, but it was just another peak that I was slowly climbing. Another high, that would lead to another low. My life was becoming a cycle of highs and lows. I mean everyone's life consists of high and lows, but mine were taken to the extremes. My highs were untouchable and my lows were unbearable.

The highs I felt so far, this year, were incredible and I'm not talking just about the drug highs. The highs that Anna gave me were better than any drug I'd done and the lows she caused pushed me to my limits. I had contemplated suicide and ended up doings pills for the first time instead.

The next few weeks would yet again test both extremes. I would dance with a different demon and experience feelings I hope I never have to feel again. All of this happened in such a short period of time during a very formative time in my life that the effects of this time never truly wore off. I would feel the effects of this time for the rest of my life. They would influence decisions that I made in the future and take me down paths I never planned to explore.

Life is nothing short of a tragic comedy and mine would prove to be no different. As I write this story, reflecting on these events bring me right back to the moment they happened and some of those feelings come flooding back. This is not an easy story for me to tell. I mean besides the fact that I'm not a writer, this story brings back emotions that have been buried for a long time. I am reexamining events that I haven't thought about for some time. Not all of them are easy to talk about for me.

That week, things went back how they used to be with Anna and me. We were spending countless hours on the phone and seeing each other as much as we could at school. That Friday, we hung out again and it was just how it used to be. I thought that I had finally made it through the nightmare and was back where I supposed to be. Everything was right in the world. Anna was back in my arms and that was all I really cared about.

That Saturday, I went over to Jake's house. It was just him and I that night. It would be our typical Saturday night. We planned to play some video games and smoke some weed. Those plans all changed though when I got a call from Anna. I answered the phone. "Hey babe."

"Heyyy."

She was fucked up. I could hear it in her voice. I didn't want to bring it up though. It didn't sound like she was on heroin. She seemed upbeat and heroin usually brings her down. It makes it sound like she's depressed. "What's up?"

"My friends having a party tonight. You guys should come."

"You do realize it's already ten?"

"Yeah, my bad. I didn't plan on coming out tonight. Since I did, I really want to see you."

I could never say no to her. "I'll see if Jake's brother can take us. I'll let you know in a little bit."

I hung up the phone and texted Jake's brother. "Yo, dude. You want to go to a party tonight?"

"Where at?"

"Octarara, it's about an hour away."

"That's kind of far."

"I'll throw you fifty bucks for gas."

"Okay, I'm down. When do you want to leave?"

"Whenever you're ready."

"I'll be down in ten. My buddy James is with me. Is it cool if he comes too?

"Yeah, that's fine."

I was excited that we were all going to a party with Anna. I had no idea whose party it was, but I was always excited to have a chance to spend time with her.

About fifteen minutes later, we all piled into Tommy's car. It was a tight fit. He drove a 1989 mustang. It was a sweet older car, but it wasn't very roomy. He turned the music up and put the address that Anna gave me into the GPS and we went on our way.

We were driving to what seemed like the middle of nowhere. There were a bunch of farms and old silos. I had never been here before and had absolutely no idea where we were.

We eventually pulled up to the address that Anna gave me. We saw two girls standing there. It was Anna and her friend. "Hey guys!" Anna shouted as we pulled up.

There were no cars at the house. It didn't look like there was any party going on here. I rolled my window down. "Is this where the parties at?"

"No, it's right down the road."

Tommy looked back at me and gave me a look. The look said what the fuck did you get us into dude. "So, I guess we're taking you there?"

"Please…." She looked at me with those puppy dog eyes that I couldn't say no to.

"Of course, hop in." We crammed two more people into the car that barely fit four people. Anna was sitting on my lap and the other girl sat on Jake's lap.

"So, where are we going?" Tommy said.

"It's life five minutes down the road, I'll direct you."

"Okay."

She started giving him directions and soon five minutes had passed and we still weren't there. It started to seem like we were driving in circles. I could tell Tommy was starting to get pissed.

"So, is there actually a party? Where are we going?"

"I just got a text, they said it got busted."

"Of course, it did." He retorted. "I'm dropping you guys back off and we're going home."

"I'm sorry you guys drove all the way out here for nothing." Anna said.

"It's cool. I guess." Was the only answer I had. I was pissed too. That I drug all these guys out here for no reason. We literally drove out here to drive around some more and go home. I was ready to go home too and call it a night.

We dropped them back off where we had picked them up. I said goodbye to Anna and we started on our way home. It was a quiet ride. I think we were all a little upset about how the night had went. We all just wanted to hurry up and get home.

My phone rang, it was Anna of course. "Hello?"

"I did something bad. Something is wrong with me."

"What did you do?"

"I took opium earlier tonight. I think I took too much."

Really? What the fuck. What was next with this girl? I thought that everything was back to normal with her. Then, she tells me she took opium. I didn't even know that you could just take opium. I thought that was something that people smoked in opium dens in China. I had no idea that you could even get opium.

"What do you want me to do?" I was done. This was my final straw. I couldn't take anymore. I had finally given up. I had no answers left for Anna. There was nothing I could do for her. Her demons had a death grip on her and they had no intention of letting go. They were far more powerful than me. I was no match for them.

"Can you come back? I want to see you."

I paused for a minute. I thought about my answer carefully This right here could be the end of us. I wanted to tread lightly, but also make it known that she no longer had control over me.

That I wasn't going to come at her every calling. She had brought me to lower places than I had ever been. She had also brought me to higher places than I'd ever been and I'd always love her for that. Yet, the lows outweighed the highs. Those lows caused me to build up a resentment towards her that would last a life time.

"No, I can't. We're almost home."

"I don't think I'm going to live. I think I'm overdosing." She whined.

"You should probably call 911 then. I can't help with that. Me coming back to see you won't solve anything."

"I want to see you one last time."

"Goodbye Anna, I hope you get the help you need."

I'm not sure what help I was referring to. It could have been in reference to her claiming she was overdosing or the help she needed to turn her life around. She was obviously in a dark place and she had brought me with her. Her demons had become my demons and I wanted to escape that dark place. I wanted to bring her with me, but she was incapable of escaping. So, I had to save myself.

I didn't want to end things with her, but I could no longer be her slave. I had to separate myself from her crazy world of drug use. I couldn't handle it. It was taking a toll on me. I had already tried pills for the first time because of it. I didn't want to continue to venture down that path.

The next morning, I texted Anna to make sure she was okay. I received a response almost immediately. She was alive. I didn't really believe that she was overdosing last night. She just wanted me to come back to her and I wanted to as well, but it wouldn't have been her that I came to see.

She wasn't the same person when she was using. It wasn't the girl I fell in love with. There was no point in going back to see that shell of a human that had been consumed by opiates.

I now could no longer believe anything the she told me. Her fake overdose made me start to question other events that had happened. Did she really go to the hospital that night after she took all those pills in front of me? Was it all just an elaborate lie? It all could have just been a cry for help. I would never know.

I don't know how she expected me to help her either. What could I possibly do for her? I couldn't take away whatever pain was causing her to feel the need to escape. I was completely powerless over the drugs.

Later that night I got a phone call from her. I answered, "Hello."

"Hey, we need to talk."

"Yeah, I think there's a lot for us to talk about."

"Why didn't you come back last night?"

Really? This was what she wanted to talk about? I couldn't believe that I was going to get reamed out for not coming back to "rescue" you her from her drug induced stupor.

"What did you want me to do? I couldn't have done anything if you were overdosing."

"I just wanted you to be there for me."

"I've been there for you through everything over the last couple months. A lot of shit has happened, but we've made it through all of it together."

"Exactly, we did it together. That's why I needed you last night."

I had nothing to say. She began to convince me that maybe I should have gone back. Maybe I should have been there for her, just to let her know that things were going to be okay. That no matter how dark the storm gets, it always passes. Yet, I didn't show up. I wasn't there to be her umbrella during the storm.

She continued, "I don't think I can do this anymore. You weren't there when I needed you. I can't stay with someone who isn't there when I need them the most."

Fuck, this was really happening. This was the end. There was no us anymore. It was just me. I'm not sure how I knew that this was really the end, I guess it was just a gut instinct. Then I slipped and words just started spewing out of my mouth.

"You fucked me up Anna, bad. Everything was so good between us in the beginning. I fell in love with someone who doesn't actually exist. Heroin became more important than me and I got put on the back burner. Heroin took you from me. It built a wall between us that I couldn't break down. That fucked with me. I didn't know what to do. You weren't there for me and I had no answers left. I wanted to die. Then, I found my answer, just like you found yours. Your answer was in a needle, mine was in a pill."

Holy shit, I told her. Why the fuck did I tell her? I just opened Pandora's box and I would never be able to shut it. Sometimes there are words that should never be spoken. What I had just told her should never have been said.

"Why would you do that?" She said angrily.

How could she be getting mad at me? She was the one shooting heroin. All I did was pop a few pills to escape for the night. "I was in a bad place and it seemed like a good idea."

"We're done. This is over. Goodbye Dan."

I didn't even get a chance to say anything. She hung up the phone before she was even finished saying my name. That was really the end. I knew it was coming sooner or later. The toxicity between was too great. We no longer positively impacted each other's lives. We only drained the life out of each other, slowly. Although, I knew it was for the best, it still hurt. It cut me deep.

Knowing that her and I would never work took me down a dark path. A darker path then I ever knew existed. So dark, that there weren't even any stars to guide my step. There was no light at the end of the path, only more darkness.

I had begun to grow up quickly because of what had happened over the last couple months. Quicker than any teenager should ever have to. I had dealt with problems that some people never deal with in their entire life. My mind didn't know how to cope with these events. My mind had already started taking me down that dark path.

The funny thing about the dark path. It doesn't look dark in the beginning. No, it's the complete opposite. It looks like a safe haven. A place that provides comfort in a way that nothing else can. That comfort comes with a price though, just like everything in life. All of our actions have consequences. I didn't know what the price tag was for that comfort that I longed for so badly. I would find out soon enough though.

The next few years of my life would be spent exploring that dark path. I guess you could say it all began that night Anna told me she was doing heroin. That was when I was introduced to a new kind of solution. It had worked for her. She had found her comfort, her warm blanket in a cold world.

For a long time, I blamed Anna for introducing me. I never felt quite right about it though, was it really her fault? Would I have ended up here no matter what? I don't know the answer to those questions, but after years of battling with the questions, I came to the conclusion that no one else can be held responsible for my own actions. She pushed me to the edge, but I was the one who decided to jump.

Chapter 6

When you take a moment to step back and think about life, it all seems very strange. The whole concept of growing and old, spending our years just watching as the clock ticks by. Life is a fickle creature. It has to be nurtured and loved, but even when it is, it can sometimes flip upside down on us. The unexpected happens and suddenly if feels like our lives were swapped with someone else's.

The strangest thing about life is death. It's the only thing in life that we our guaranteed. Yet, for some reason we fear it. It scares us because in life there are only so many possibilities. In death, there are endless possibilities. We don't know what awaits us. Some believe that it is heaven or hell, some believe that we are reincarnated and some believe that there is nothing after this. There are countless beliefs about what awaits us once we take our final breath.

I'm not sure what I believe. I want to believe that there is something greater out there, but it just seems illogical to me. There are too many ways for me to justify why there just couldn't possibly be a "god," but that's a topic for another time.

Death is the end of our stories. Life is that little hyphen on our gravestones that represents everything that we have ever done. It represents our time in this world. Death is the period at the end of our sentence.

Soon I would look death in the eyes for the first time. I would see it's face. Death would look back at me with a wry smile, letting me know that my time hadn't come yet. This would be just my first brush with death. I would look into its eyes and see the darkness that lay within them.

My brush with death would make me feel more alive than ever. It was a different kind of high. One that was caused by getting so closed to death that I could feel its breath on my cheek. I could feel the coldness that hit my cheek as it exhaled. Yet, somehow I was able to survive.

Anna and I were officially done and I didn't know how to cope with that fact. I had lost the one person in this world that had meant everything to me. She was the reason that I woke up in the morning and the reason that I smiled before falling asleep. Without her, I didn't know what to do. I didn't know how to go on.

The only answer that I had was to resort to pills. They made me feel numb. They gave me a comfort that I couldn't find on my own. They answered questions that I didn't even know I had. So, I started taking them more often. It started as just on the weekends, then it spilled over to taking them in school. I was slowly sliding a cliff that I couldn't get a grasp on.

Anna and I still talked all the time, but it wasn't the same. I think we still talked because we had so much history together. We weren't together that long, but so much has happened in that short period of time. She had moved on and started seeing someone else, it was actually one of my best friends from grade school. It didn't really bother me though. For some reason, I believed that he could never have her in the way that I had her. At the end of the night, I was still the person that she called. I was still the person she found comfort in.

Even though we still talked. I was mentally fucked up. The pills had become my coping mechanism. They were my escapee from reality. They allowed me to find peace for a brief period of time.

I had started taking them a few times a week during school. It made the day go by faster and kept my mind off of Anna. Slowly, people started to notice I was acting different. I don't think anyone knew what I was doing because I kept that fact to myself. I didn't need people knowing that I had become a pill head. I didn't need that stain on my reputation. Yet, people knew something was wrong.

One day, I was walking through the halls, I had taken eight pills that morning so I was pretty fucked up. Anna was at her locker. I stopped to talk to her. "Hey Anna." She looked up from her locker at me and I could see the life drain out of her face. She knew exactly what was going on. She could tell I was fucked up. I usually tried to avoid her when I was on, but for some reason my mind told me to try to talk to her that day."

"You're scaring me."

My mind was racing. I know that when I'm on my eyes get super glassy and my pupils get really engorged. It kind of gives me this crazy look in my eyes. She saw that look and knew exactly what it was. She didn't know what kind of pills I was taking, but she knew I was fucked up. "How am I scaring you?"

"You need some help. I should tell somebody what you're doing."

She slammed her locker and walked away. I watched as she walked away. How could she do this to me? How could she leave me in my time of need? This was exactly why we had broken up because I had left her in her time of need. Now she was doing the exact same thing to me.

I didn't know what to do. I was angry at her, but my emotions were still numb. The pills were blocking any feelings that I would have had. I didn't even care that she threatened to tell somebody what was going on. I mean, I knew that she never would, but still the threat of it should have put a little fear in me. It didn't. When I was high, I had no emotion, no fear, no care in the world. I was sufficiently numb.

I now knew that when I was high I had to avoid Anna completely. I didn't want her to know what I was doing. Even though it was her fault that I was taking these pills. If we never dated, I never would have felt the need to escape. My life would have continued on perfectly fine. I would have never been introduced to drugs and the comforting effect they had on me. I would have had no need for them. She was the cause of this.

She called me that night. "Hey."

"We need to talk. I can't handle seeing you like that."

"Like what?" I played dumb. I didn't want to own up to what I was doing.

"You're getting high. I don't know what the fuck you're doing, but I know you were fucked up today. I've been hearing shit from other people and I didn't want to believe it, but when I saw you today I could tell."

"Yeah, you're right. I've been taking pills here and there."

"What kind of pills?" She said in the most accusing voice I had ever heard.

"What does it matter? I'm getting fucked up and I'm going to continue to get fucked up."

"Why are you doing this?"

That question set me off. How did she have the nerve to ask me that. She had to know damn well why I was doing this. It was her. She had led me to the edge and pushed me off. She led me to the pills. How could she not see that?

"You're fucking kidding me, right? You tried to kill yourself after you thought you had gotten pregnant. Literally, while I watched. You actually overdosed and had to get taken to the hospital. Then, you tell me you're a heroin addict. Oh, and on top of that you tell me the other night that you think you're overdosing again. How the fuck do you expect me to handle that? Well, I'll tell you. I'm handling it the same way you do when life seems too heavy. You shoot heroin and I pop pills. We're both fucked up."

"I don't know what to say to you. I'm sorry I guess."

"You should be. I'm taking these pills because of you. You did this to me."

"Please don't say that."

Her voice shook as she said that. I could hear that she was starting to cry. I didn't even care. I needed her to know the pain that I was feeling because of her. She had caused that pain and I felt that she should feel some of it too. It was only right that we felt that pain together.

"It's the truth and I'm sorry if that hurts you, but that's just how it is."

"I want you to know something."

"What?"

"I love you and I will always love you no matter what. You are heading down a path that I don't want you to go down. Heroin has taken me places I never wanted to go. Please, don't follow me down that path."

"I love you too. I'm going to go now."

I hung up the phone and stared at the wall. I was thinking about everything that had just been said. I regretted it. I didn't want to hurt her and I know everything I said killed her inside. She knew exactly where I was heading and wanted to try to stop me, but she knew she couldn't. Just like I couldn't stop her from shooting heroin. We both had pain that couldn't be taken away except by a substance. We had both found our solution.

I'll never forget that look in her eyes when she saw me all fucked up. It still haunts me to this day. It's like my eyes told a story that my words never could. She learned more about me from one glance then I could ever tell her. My eyes told my story for me. They expressed the pain that I was in.

I always wonder about that day. What if she had told somebody? Would I have stopped getting high? Maybe I would have found a different coping mechanism. Who knows. I also wonder if I had handled it differently would we have fought our demons together. We could have vowed to both stop getting high and trying to find the comfort that we once had in each other again.

Those questions kept me up at night for a long time. It's funny how seemly insignificant events have such a profound impact on our lives. There are many of these instances that happen in my life. That if I had done something different maybe I wouldn't be sitting here telling you this story or maybe I would and it would just have a different ending.

Anna and I had stopped talking to each other. There was really nothing left to say. We were both in a fucked up place and couldn't dig ourselves out of it. We were just two lost souls looking for an answer that we would never find.

Easter break was coming up and I was going to be spending the weekend at one of my friend's house because my parents were going away. The night before my parents were leaving, Jake, Chris and I decided to go out. Chris was a friend of Jake's. I had only met him a few times.

Tonight, we were going to go carring. Carring was breaking into people's cars and taking whatever we could find. I guess, I shouldn't say breaking in. We would only go into cars that were left unlocked. It was something fun for us to do. It provided a certain rush that I couldn't achieve through anything else and it put some extra money in my pocket.

That night, Jake was going to wait until his parents went to sleep and take his moms car. We were going to get Chris and head back to my neighborhood to ransack some cars. We had never done this as a group before, I had only done it by myself. I thought it might be more fun if I had some company though.

It was about one in the morning when my phone rang. "Hello."

"Yo dude! I'm driving! I'm on my way to your house. I'll be there in a few!"

"Hell yeah! I'll meet you a couple houses down. You'll see me."

I hung up the phone and got dressed. I put on black sweatpants and a black hoodie so it would be harder to see me. I didn't want to be able to be spotted easily since we were going to be robbing cars.

Once I was dressed, I opened up the window and climbed out onto the roof. I was going out this way because I didn't want my parents to hear me going downstairs. Once I was on the roof, I walked over to the edge and dangled my feet off to make the fall a little easier. I thought about it for a second than propelled my body off the roof. As I hit the grass, I rolled to break my fall. It must have looked like I was James Bond. I thought I pulled it off very smoothly because it didn't hurt at all.

Once I gathered myself, I walked to the top of my driveway and started walking down the sidewalk. I didn't want to get picked up in front of my house just in case someone happened to see me. Then I saw headlights come up over the hill. I ducked down behind a tree just in case it wasn't

Jake. As the car got closer, I could see that it was Jake's mom's car.

I stepped out from behind the tree as the car came to a stop in front of me. I opened the door and hopped in. "Holy shit dude, I can't believe you actually took the car!"

"It's wild, I can't believe I'm driving! This is so fucking cool. You ready to go get Chris?"

"Yeah, let's go!"

He started driving to Chris's house. He only lived about five minutes away. There were no other cars on the road. He obeyed all the traffic laws because we definitely did not want to get pulled over. We would have been in so much trouble. We were pretty quiet during the car ride. I think we were just enjoying the moment.

We pulled up to Chris's house and Jake called him. A few moments later, he walked out, dressed in all black and hopped in the back seat. "What's up boys!"

"You ready to go make some money!"

"Hell yeah, let's do this shit. Where are we going?"

"We're going to head back to my neighborhood. There's a ton of houses and there's never any cops so we should have no issues."

"Sounds like a plan."

We started the trek back to my neighborhood. Once we got there, I directed Jake where he should park the car. We all mapped out what streets we were going to hit and that we would meet back at the car in fifteen minutes. With our plans in order, we all hopped out and went our separate ways.

The first few cars I tried were all locked. Finally, I found an open one and started going through the car. There were a few bucks in the center console, nothing in the glove box, except for some tissues. I noticed something in the door handle out of the corner of my eye. I reached down and grabbed it. It was a wallet. I flipped it open and took all the money that was in it. Then, an outdoor light flipped on. I closed the door and made a run for it. I ran about a half a block before I jumped into some bushes to make sure I was in the clear.

I looked back at the driveway I was just in. No one had come outside. I must have activated the motion sensor light. "What a shitty light," I laughed to myself. I can't believe I didn't set it off when I walked up. I waited a few minutes before stepping out of the bush just to be on the safe side.

I reached into my pocket to check my phone to see what time it was. It had already been about fifteen minutes so I started heading back to the car. When I got there, Jake and Chris still weren't back. So, I hopped behind a bush to wait for them.

After a few minutes, I saw the two of them walking back together. They were carrying a few items. I stepped out of the bush and waved to them. As they got closer, I could see they were holding two six packs of soda and some electronics. "Really? You guys took soda?"

"Yeah, it's going to be a long night so we're probably going to get thirsty."

I rolled my eyes. My friends were idiots. "What else did you get?"

"We got an iPod, DVD player and some cash. You get anything good?"

I pulled the money out of my pocket and started counting it. "Looks like I got about one hundred dollars."

"That was a good start to the night! I think we got about sixty."

"Hell yeah. Let's head to the neighborhood behind mine."

We threw the soda and electronics in the back seat. All of the money we stuffed into the center console. I hopped back up front and Chris hopped in the back. Jake started the car and started driving out of my neighborhood. The quickest way to get to the neighborhood behind mine was by going back to the street I lived on and taking that road out of my neighborhood.

Once we turned onto my street. Jake floored the gas pedal. The car started accelerating quickly. "What are you doing?"

"I want to hit a hundred."

I glanced over at the speedometer and saw that we were going eighty already. I figured that he would hit a hundred and slow down. The car kept accelerating as we went over the crest of the hill. Jake must have forgot that my road has a bit of a turn in it. He realized this as soon as we went over the peak.

He pressed the breaks, but the car was not stopping quick enough. We were quickly approaching the bend in the road. At that point, I realized that he wasn't going to be able to keep the car on the road. We were going to crash. There was a creek at the bottom of the hill and we were headed straight for it.

Jake continued to slam on the breaks in hopes that the car would stop. The tires hit the curb and we jumped up into the grass. The car slammed through a mailbox with ease. We were still going pretty fast and I knew that we were going to end up in the creek. All three of us were dead silent. There were no screams, we all knew what was happening and we braced ourselves for impact.

My mind went into survival mode. I started to reach up in an attempt to put my seat belt on and then decided that I would never have time to put the buckle in place. Instead, I curled up in a ball and hit the floor. I positioned myself where you typically put your feet. We were only about twenty yards from the creek at that point. I knew the impact was coming.

Then it happened. It sounded like a bomb went off. The car came to an abrupt stop and my mind was now in escape mode. I knew I had survived the crash. Now, I needed to get the fuck out of there before anyone else showed up.

I reached for the door and pulled the handle, but the door was jammed shut. The passenger window had broken during the accident, so I climbed through the window. Once I was outside of the car, my legs started moving. I was running, running faster than I ever had before. I didn't know where I was running to, but I just had to get away from that car.

I ran about three hundred yards before I stopped in someone's driveway to look behind me.

I had totally forgot to check to see if my friends were okay. When I turned around, I saw Jake and Chris about halfway to where I was. Jake had some things in his arms. I waited for them to catch up to me.

"You two good?"

"I think so."

"Why did you grab all the stuff?"

"I didn't want the cops to find out we were stealing stuff when they find the car."

"HEY!" A voice shouted from the house behind us. Without hesitation, the three of us took off running. We ran into the woods that were behind the house and kept running until we couldn't see the houses anymore. Someone must have heard the crash and came out to see what had happened. We weren't sticking around to answer any questions.

"What are we going to do?" I said.

"We're all going to go home and pretend like nothing happened," Jake replied.

"How the fuck are we going to do that?"

"We're all going to walk home and climb into bed. When the cops come to my house, I'll play dumb and they'll assume someone stole the car. The two of you walk home and just go to bed."

"Okay."

I started walking through the woods back to my house and the two of them started walking back home. Jake didn't have too far of a walk, but Chris was going to have a long walk home. I had the shortest.

Once I was back at my house. I went around to the back and slowly slid open the sliding door, doing my best not to make a sound. When I got in, I looked down at my shirt and saw blood on it. I didn't know where I was bleeding from so I headed into the bathroom.

I took a look in the mirror and saw that my braces had gone through my lip. The adrenaline from the crash must have pumping so hard that I couldn't feel the pain. What the fuck was I going to do? My braces were stuck in my lip and I definitely needed stitches.

I had to think fast. The best solution I came up with was to throw a pair of shoes down the stairs and act like I had fallen. There was no way I could tell my parents what happened and this seemed like the best solution.

I walked upstairs and grabbed a pair of shoes. I went back to the stairs and walked halfway down. From there, I threw my shoes down the stairs and ran after them. When I reached the bottom, I threw my body down against the floor to make as much noise as I possibly could.

It worked, I heard my mom yell, "Dan!" She came running out of her room and saw me laying at the bottom of the stairs. She rushed down. "What happened?"

"I was coming down to get a drink and I must have slipped. My lip hurts."

"It looks like you cut it really bad. Go look in the mirror and see if you're okay."

I pulled myself up off the ground slowly and limped my way into the bathroom. I already knew that my braces were stuck in my lip. Now, I just had to go back out there and tell my mom that I need to go get stitches.

I walked back out. "Mom, my braces are stuck in my lip. I think we need to go to the hospital."

"Okay, honey. Let me go get dressed really quickly."

It worked! I was going to get my lip fixed and I avoided getting caught. There was only one more problem. The quickest way to get to the hospital was by taking the road that we had just crashed the car on. I needed an excuse to tell my mom to take a different way out. I figured I would tell her that I think one of the neighbors are moving and to see if there is a sale sign up yet.

As we were getting in the car, I asked, "I think the Taylors are moving. Can we drive past and see if the house is up for sale?"

"Sure."

It was an odd request at four in the morning, but my mom complied and took a different route out of the neighborhood. I was in the clear. Somehow, I managed to get through that night without getting in trouble.

That was my first brush with death. None of us had our seatbelts on and we went off the road at eighty miles an hour. I had a near death experience, there was no light or slow-motion reel of events that had happened. What did happen, was my mind and body fought for survival. It's the most basic human instinct and when I was in danger, that was how I reacted. There was no fear of death. Just a battle to survive the next few seconds.

That night changed my views about death. I no longer feared death. I accepted it. It was the only promise that life gave me. I knew that one day I would inevitably meet my final moments. My fear of death was gone, but it was replaced by a deep respect for death. I had flirted with death, but it wasn't my time.

Jake ended up getting caught. I'll finish that story in the next chapter. I needed to tell you this because of what the cops told him. They told him that we should have all died in that car that night. Jake didn't tell them that anyone was with him, but they could tell from all the airbags deploying that other people were in the car. They told him he was lucky to be alive and that he hadn't hurt or killed anyone.

We were all given a second chance that night. We all were able to walk away from that accident with only a few minor bumps and bruises. Well, also the few stitches in my lip. I don't think any of us would ever forget that night. It was a night that we all could have died, yet for some reason, death didn't want to take us.

Chapter 7

The next day, I slept in pretty late. I woke up around ten in the morning. We didn't have school that day because it was Good Friday. Our Easter vacation had begun. Slowly, the memory of last night flooded back into my head. I realized we had crashed Jake's mom's car and I had stitches in my lip from the accident. I grabbed my phone and called Jake.

"Yo dude. How'd everything go last night?"

"Well, I got home and went to bed. A little while later, the cops showed up at my house. They came and got me out of bed. I denied everything at first, but then they told me that the keys had been left in the car. They knew I took it, so I owned up to it."

"Did you mention anything about Chris and I?"

"No, they asked me if anyone else was in the car. I told them that it was just me. They said since the passenger airbag went off, they knew someone else was in the car. I just kept denying it though."

"You're the fucking man. I ended up having to go get stitches in my lip last night. My braces were stuck in my lip. I didn't even realize until I got home."

"How'd you pull that off?"

"I pretended to fall down the stairs."

"That was smart as shit, but I'm pretty sure my mom called your mom since I crashed in your neighborhood. She thinks you were with me."

"Well, I'm just going to deny the shit out of it. My parents can't prove I was in the car."

"Good luck."

I hung up the phone and prepared myself to go down stairs and face my mom. She was going to accuse me of being in that car, which she wasn't wrong about. I was going to have to stick to my story and hope it worked.

I finally gathered up the courage to head downstairs. I walked into the kitchen and my mom was making food for herself. "Hey bud."

"Good morning mom."

"So, I need to ask you something."

"Shoot." I knew what was coming.

"Are you sure you fell down the stairs last night?"

"Um, yeah. Why?" I mustered the most confused look that I possibly could.

"Well, I just got a call from Mrs. Crane. She said that Jake took her car last night and he crashed it in our neighborhood."

"Are you serious? That's crazy."

"Yeah, she called me a little bit ago. Apparently, he crashed it into the Prator's yard. It was a pretty bad accident. He's okay though."

"Wow, I'm glad he's okay. I'll have to call him and find out what happened."

"I find it to be too much of a coincidence that around the same that he crashed the car, you fell down the stairs and busted your lip."

"I don't know what to tell you mom. I'm sure stranger things have happened."

"Yeah, I guess."

I could tell she was pissed. She knew I was in that car, but she couldn't prove it. There was really nothing she could do. She couldn't punish me over an eerie coincidence and I'm sure she truly hoped I wasn't in that car. She accepted it for what it was and somehow that was the end of it.

My parents and I had a very good relationship up until this point. This was the beginning of me separating my life from them I now had a huge secret that I could never tell them, even if in their hearts, they knew the truth.

Over the next year, I would try to sever my relationship completely with them. I would become someone that they didn't recognize and there was nothing they could have done to avoid it. My life choices had lead me down a path that they could not steer me off of. They were powerless and it broke their hearts.

The only regrets I have in my life are how I treated my parents over the next few years. They had done nothing to deserve the anguish that I would be putting them through. I would say things that I now wish I could take back, but some words can never be unsaid.

Anna and I had started talking again. She was seeing someone else, yet again. He was two years older than us. He went to the same high school. I had heard his name before, but never really knew who he was. As always, Anna still came back to me though. She could have another interest in her life, but she couldn't stay away from me for good. Something just kept pulling her back. Neither of us could walk away.

It was the perfect breeding ground for a completely toxic relationship. She was still getting high. She had stopped shooting heroin though. She had gone back to doing pills. She was now doing OxyContin. Apparently, one of her friends was a pretty big dealer and were giving her shit for free every week. I didn't really know too much about Oxy, but I figured it was better than her shooting heroin.

I was still getting high on DXM every chance I got. I was taking them at school and on the weekends. They were my only escape. They gave me a chance to feel normal for a little while. They quieted the voices in my head and allowed me to feel nothing.

Anna and I no longer spent our Fridays together, she was spending them with her new boyfriend. I still got to see her though. Jake's brother, Tommy, was taking me to her house at night about once a week. We would head there in the middle of the night and I would climb up onto her roof and sneak in through the window. I would spend the night and he would come back to get me in the morning. I was paying him for the service, but it was worth every penny so that I could spend nights with her.

Our nights spent together consisted of watching movies, talking and having sex. When we were together, everything was right in the world. I had no desire to get high because I found peace with her. Even with everything else going on, it was like when we were together all of our problems faded away and disappeared for a little while.

It was almost like we pretended nothing was wrong. We pretended that she hadn't tried to kill herself. We pretended that she wasn't doing Oxys. We pretended that I wasn't popping pills. We pretended that she didn't have a boyfriend. We were living in a world that didn't actually exist. We had created this space where we locked all of reality on the outside and we huddled on the inside. It was our sacred space and we weren't going to let anything ruin that.

I was going over her house about once a week. It was always a weekend night. I would tell my parents that I was staying over a friend's house, when I was actually going over Anna's. Her parents never came into her room and they were always out and about for the day by the time we would wake up. So, we would hang out for a little while, then Tommy would come to pick me up. I was actually really enjoying the system we had created.

We spent the rest of the school year going on like that. Anna dated other people and I kept on getting high. I wasn't getting high because of Anna anymore. I was getting high because I wanted to. The pills had become second nature to me. They had helped me through dark times and it felt wrong to sever that bond. They were there for me when no one else was. They made me feel right, when everything in the world was wrong. They were my best friends.

There was only one more incident with Anna during the school year. She called me on a Saturday night. "Hello?"

"Dan, I think I'm dying." She was sobbing and her breathing sounded exasperated.

"What did you take?"

"I think I did too much Oxy."

"What do you want me to do?"

"Can you please come over and be with me?"

I thought for a moment. I did love seeing her and spending time with her, but I couldn't be her lifeline. If she was actually overdosing, there was nothing I could do. I think she just was crying out for help. I was happy that I was the one she called and not her boyfriend, but I didn't want to see Anna in that state.

We both had kept our drug use away from one another. She did her thing and I did mine. We were never fucked up when we were around each other. That kept the illusion going that everything was okay with the both of us. Neither of us could handle seeing each other all fucked up.

"I can't do that Anna. I can't come to the rescue every time you do a little too much."

"I need you."

"There's nothing I can do for you. Call your boyfriend."

I hung up the phone. Anna had yet again cried wolf about overdosing. I knew she wasn't. The only time she had overdosed and ended up in the hospital, I didn't receive a call until afterwards. Now, I knew better. I wasn't going to be her knight in shining armor that came to save the princess in distress. I couldn't be that for her.

I couldn't even help myself, so how did she expect me to help her? We were both in the same dark place, clawing to get out, but only digging ourselves deeper. We had ventured down a path that had no fairy tale ending. Life isn't all happy endings you know.

The movies that you watch with the happy endings are all just made up stories. This is real life. The fairy tale endings we were all told as children aren't real. When you finally realize that most stories don't have a happy ending, you can accept a lot more about life. You learn to take the good with the bad and the beautiful with the ugly. You learn that most stories aren't about a happy ending. They are about learning a lesson. Something that you can carry with you the rest of your life and base future decisions on the lessons you've learned.

Our story of us, is a just another tragic love story. It's not the love story that your parents told you of how they met. It's more like Romeo and Juliet, if they were both drug addicts.

That night I came to a realization that Anna and I were exactly the same. Our demons had consumed us and our toxic relationship was the only semblance of reality that we clung too. We were each other's life lines to the real world. We were each other's reason to cling on to life.

Summer came around and things with Anna took a turn for the worse. I had taken a whole box of pills that night. I had just recently started doubling the dose. Before, I was only taking half of the box. That wasn't really doing the job anymore.

Taking a whole box took me a whole new level of numbness.

That night, Anna called me. "Hello."

"I'm fucked up."

"Me too."

"I'm like really fucked up and want to see you."

I was too high for this shit again. Why did she always do this to me? She still wanted me to be the person to rescue her. I couldn't deal with shit again.

"I'm way too high for this."

"Are you fucking kidding me? You're supposed to be there for me when I need you the most."

"That's funny, I thought that was your boyfriend's job."

"You have always been there for me, why are you doing this to me now?"

"It's hard to deal with you when you're all fucked up and it's impossible to deal with you when I'm all fucked up too. There's just no way we can benefit each other when we're both high."

"I just want to talk to you. I want you to be there and comfort me when I'm hurting."

"You get you're comfort from the Oxy, what do you need me for?"

"I Just told you, I just want to talk to you. Hearing your voice comforts me. It brings me back to when we first met and none of the craziness had happened yet."

"Well, I'm too fucked up. I just want to chill and play video games."

"I fucking loved you Dan. I don't know why you're treating me like this now."

"I told you. I'm fucked up."

"That's not a good answer."

"Goodbye Anna."

Had I finally reached my end with her? I didn't think so. I was just really high and not in any state to be talking to her. Was I too harsh on her? Maybe. It wasn't me talking anymore though, the drugs were doing the talking for me. I hope she saw that. I hope she was able to see past the drug induced words that were falling out of my mouth and see the person that was begging for help behind them. Maybe she couldn't though.

Shortly after that night, my family and I headed down the beach for vacation. I was happy to get away from home for a little bit and spend some time just relaxing on the beach with my family. What I didn't know, was that my life was about to get flipped upside down.

The first night that we were there, I received a phone call from Anna. I stepped outside to take the call. "Hey."

"Dan, we need to talk."

"About what?" I thought she was going to say we needed to talk about us. That we couldn't keep doing what we were doing.

"There's something I need to tell you. It's been killing me and I can't keep it from you any longer."

I had no idea what she was going to tell me. "Okay."

"I had an abortion last month. It was yours. I'm so sorry." She broke down crying.

I had no words. There was nothing that I could say. I broke down crying too. The reason it hit me so hard was because I was adopted. My birth parents had set up an adoption for me the day I was born. I had my new parents waiting to receive me and my birth parents waiting to give me up. My birth parents were very young, they were only eighteen. They believed that they were making the right decision in putting me up for adoption.

The fact that I was adopted never bothered me. My adopted parents were the only parents I ever knew. I loved them like they were actually the ones who had given birth to me. I held no animosity towards my birth parents giving me away. They gave me to a loving family and I thanked them for that.

The reason that this hit me so hard was because my birth parents could have gotten an abortion. They could have decided to take my life and never give me a chance. They chose to go through the pregnancy so that their child could have a chance in life. They wanted to put that life out into the world and see what that life could become.

Anna broke the silence, "I didn't know how to tell you Dan. I got pregnant at some point and didn't know what to do. An abortion seemed like my only option. I had one of my friends take me to have the procedure done. They made me listen to the heartbeat. It was horrible. I hate myself for it."

"Why didn't you tell me before? I know in the end it would have been your decision, but we could have at least talked about it. You know I'm adopted and that this would fuck me up."

"That's why I didn't want to tell you. I didn't want to put this burden on you."

"Well, you did now."

"I know. I felt like you had a right to know and I just couldn't hold it in any longer."

"I can't believe you did this."

"I'm so sorry. Now, we have an angel watching over us. I named her Ava."

Really? This bitch had the audacity to tell me she killed our child without me knowing and she went ahead and named her. That pushed me over the edge. I was fucking done. I didn't want anything to do with her anymore. This was my final straw. People can only be pushed so far before they break and she finally broke me.

"I can't do this anymore. I don't want to talk to you anymore. Please, don't call me ever again." I hung up the phone.

My mind was racing. I had finally reached my breaking point. I wanted to get fucked up. I wanted to not feel this pain. I just wanted to be numb. I wanted to forget everything about Anna. I hated her. I fucking hated her for what she had done. I could accept the drugs, the other guys, but not this. She had gone too far. I could never forgive her for this.

That was the end of us. That was our fairy tale ending. It ended in death. There was no happy love song at the end of the film. Just feelings of betrayal and hate. It's funny how you can think you love a person and grow to hate them. It was a weird feeling for me though because I still loved her too. I didn't love the lying drug addict that she turned into, but I loved the person that I met on New Year's Eve.

I had to get away from Anna. I had to put as much distant as I possibly could between us. I knew if we were in close proximity to each other that we would be drawn back together. I didn't know how I was going to do this, but I knew I absolutely had to. I couldn't go on dealing with her and the emotional pain she caused me.

This was my second encounter with death. This time death took a different form. It wasn't my life that death had come for. It was our child's life. Actually, death didn't even come for Ava. Anna caused the death. She was the one that took that life. My child would be eleven right now if Anna hadn't taken her life. I would probably be picking her up from school right now, talking to her about how her day was. We would be laughing and talking about what we would be having for dinner. My life would be completely different.

Chapter 8

They say with every ending there is a new beginning. Yet, sometimes those new beginnings lead us to places we never wanted to go. We take steps down roads that we can never retrace. Our footprints will always be there. We will leave our mark on that road and that road will leave its mark on us. Our footprints tell stories that our words never could. They tell us where we've been and where we are heading. Yet, they can't tell us where the road leads. We are left to decide how far down the road we want to travel.

Anna and I were done. I didn't want to be done though. I still wanted her, but I wanted the old her. The girl I had first met, not the person she was now. She had become someone I didn't even recognize anymore. Her actions left scars on me that would last a lifetime.

I still could not wrap my mind around what she had done. I couldn't figure out why she hadn't told me and went ahead and had an abortion without my knowledge. I know I couldn't have changed her mind, but I felt like I had the right to know about it. I was struggling dealing with the fact that she killed our child.

I had to get away from her, as far away as possible. The first thought that came into my head was that I was going to have to change schools. This was the only way that I could escape her. I knew that if I went back to my school she would find her way back to me. She was like a drug and I was addicted. I needed to go cold turkey.

I decided that was what was best for me. I had made some friends that went to the local public school and that was where I wanted to go. I would already have some friends there and best of all, I would be far away from Anna. I wouldn't have to pass her in the hallways or see her in any shape or form. I could truly distance myself and be free of her grasp for the first time since we met.

Once my mind was made up. I told my parents over dinner. "So, I want to talk to you guys about something."

"What's going on?"

"I don't want to go about to Pius. I want to go to Perkiomen Valley."

"What? Are you sure you really want to do that?"

"Yeah, things just aren't working out. I think I would be better off at a new school."

"We're only going to ask this one more time. Are you sure this is what you think is best for you?"

"I've thought about it a lot and I think that this is the best decision for me."

"Okay, we'll figure out what we have to do to get you transferred."

"Thanks guys. I love you."

"You know we love you too."

That was way easier than I had anticipated. They barely asked any questions. I think they knew why I wanted to switch schools and knew me well enough to not ask too many questions. I don't like talking about girls or my feelings about them to my parents. They have accepted that and just avoided the topic. I think they knew that Anna was the reason for me leaving.

That was it. That was the grand finale for Anna and I. I had chosen to end our toxic relationship, but even though I was the one to walk away, I was still hurting bad. She had taken a piece of me that she would hold onto forever. Part of my heart would be left with her and I would be left with an empty part of myself. The only thing that helped to fill that emptiness was my pills.

I knew I couldn't keep taking them though. If I did, I was no better than Anna. I vowed to myself that I would stop. I would still smoke weed, but I was going to stay away from those fucking pills. Sure, they gave me comfort and provided me an escape, but it was only temporary. If I was ever going to get over Anna, I would have to find a way to fix myself in a healthy manner.

I didn't tell anyone that I wasn't going back to my old school. I didn't want Anna to know. It would be a surprise to everyone when I wasn't there on the first day of class. I thought that if Anna found out, she would try to convince me to come back. I knew that I was powerless over her and I would end up giving in and going back to school with her. So, I kept it to myself.

The summer went on and Anna would call me here and there. I would listen as the phone rang and let it go to voicemail. I was trying with everything in me to let go of her. I knew talking to her would just cause all of the emotions to come flooding back. Ignoring her was the only thing I could do.

The rest of the summer was spent hanging out with my friends. We would play sports and hang out. None of us had jobs since we were so young. So, the summer was a care free time for us.

I still was drinking and smoking weed with my friends, but it was different. I wasn't doing it to escape. We were just getting fucked up for fun. I wasn't using it to run from my emotions. It was just something fun for us to do.

All my pain had been bottled up and pushed deep down. I was doing my best to keep myself busy with my friends. As long as my mind was occupied, I was okay. It was the late nights when I had no one to talk to that she would come creeping into my mind. I would struggle with everything that had happened. I would fantasize about us getting back together and living happily ever after, but it was just a fantasy. I knew it would never happen. There was no happy ending for us.

Ava always pops into my mind too. I would think about how far along Anna would have been and how much longer I would have to wait to meet my child. I would think about the life she could have had. The life that was taken away without me even knowing. That was what caused me the greatest pain.

I got through those nights though. I would listen to music and get lost in the music. I even started writing music myself. It was an outlet for me, a healthy outlet. It allowed me to express myself. I never showed the music to anyone, but it was something that allowed me to write down how I was feeling. It allowed me to let go of some of the things that happened.

I was beginning to develop healthy coping mechanisms, between my friends and music, I was doing okay. I wasn't great, but I no longer felt the need to take pills. The pills never really even crossed my mind. It was like that had become so far removed from my life that they no longer seemed to be an option for me. I felt proud of myself for that.

I had gotten so wrapped up in the pills, just like Anna had been wrapped up in heroin. It had become my only escape, but for the time being I had relinquished them from my life. I was slowly moving on from the pills and Anna.

As the new school year drew closer, I was getting excited. I was ready for a new chapter in my life, the one that Anna would be absent from. I didn't know what the new school year had in store for me, but I was sure that it was going to be better than my freshmen year. There would be new faces and new classes. Everything would be new to me. The slate was wiped clean and I was ready to start over.

I wasn't going to play any sports this year though. My freshmen year I got hurt pretty bad playing football. I had broken my collarbone and tore two joints in my shoulder. That happened early on in the season and I didn't play anymore that year. I was done.

That spring I tried to play baseball. The arm that I injured was my throwing arm and I was a pitcher. I was never able to throw the ball the same after my injury. I knew that sports at a high school level were no longer going to be a part of my life. That was a tough pill for me to swallow.

My dream from a young age was to become a professional baseball player. I dreamed of being on the mound pitching while the crowd cheered for me as I struck out a batter. That dream was now broken.

Although there would be no sports for me, there were still plenty of things to look forward to at school. I was always pretty intelligent, so I had been placed in honors classes at my new school. I planned to focus on school and work on getting into a good college.

That next year did not go as planned, just like everything else in my life. The next year would take me to lower lows and higher highs. I would meet new people and experiment with new drugs. I would find love again and I would be crushed again.

This was another point in my life where I wonder what would have happened had I not changed schools. Would I still have fell in with the same group of friends? Would I still do all the same drugs? Would I have gotten back together with Anna? I don't know, but it was a major turning point in my life and I turned the wrong way.

When you make a turn in life, sometimes there's no going back. You can't undo what's been done and said. There is no restart button. I thought there was. I thought that going to a new school would be like resetting the game, I was wrong.

Chapter 9

My new beginning had finally come. I was at a new school and was ready to start over. I was as far away from Anna as I could possibly be. I was in a new place with new people and whatever happened now would all be of my own doing. Anna no longer had control of my life. I was free, but the thoughts still lingered.

I was trying so hard to start over, but my mind wouldn't let me. Once the school year started, I started sinking into a dark place. My mind was retreating into its own depths. I began isolating myself. I wasn't making any new friends at school. It was because I wasn't trying. I didn't talk to anybody there except the few friends I already had at the school. I wasn't interested in meeting new people. That was too hard for me. It wasn't that I wasn't outgoing, my mind just wasn't allowing me to let any new people into my life.

I think it was because the last time I let someone new into my life, they destroyed it. So, my mind started building walls to keep everyone out. It was a defense mechanism to keep me from getting hurt again. If I didn't let anyone new into my life, there was no possibility to get hurt.

My friends at my new school consisted of a core group of five guys. There were a few other people that I was friendly with, only because my friends were friends with them. The five guys that I considered my closest friends were Mikey, Brian, Kevin, Tyler and Chris. If you don't remember, Mikey was the one who told Jake and I about the

DXM pills. He was the one who introduced us to them.

I was really close with these guys. We would hang out every day after school. All my free time was spent with them. We would go to Chris's house after school and smoke weed for a few hours until his parents got home. They had to know that we smoked weed because we smoked in the house and it had to reek of weed when they came home. For whatever reason, they never said anything to him about it.

So, that became my daily routine. I would go to school miserable and spend the day just waiting for the final bell to ring. Once the bell rang, the rest of my night consisted of getting high and hanging out with my friends.

Things were about to change yet again. My mind was still in a dark place, even will Anna out of the picture. I was still struggling with all the emotional damage she had caused. All of that pain was bottled up. I didn't talk about it to anyone. I just couldn't. I couldn't bring myself to tell anyone all of the craziness that had happened with her.

Emotions can only stay bottled up for so long before they explode. My emotions were boiling and it was only a matter of time before my life would become mayhem again. My demons would come back and they would win the battle, but the war would continue.

Jake called me. "Yo, dude."
"What's up?"
"I got some new shit for us to try?"

"What did you get?"

"I copped some OxyContins from Mark."

"What? No way. How many milligrams?"

"Eighty. There the good ones."

"Hell yeah. We doing it tomorrow?"

"You know it! I know I still owe you some money so we can split the pill and we'll call it even."

"That's cool by me."

To say I was excited, would be an understatement. I had seen what Oxy did for Anna and god did I want to try it. I hadn't done any pills for about four months and was craving to feel numb again. Oxy's are opiates, so it would be the first time that I would try an opiate. Opiates are considered downers and I was used to doing dissociatives, so it would be a new experience for me.

I only had to wait until tomorrow. Tomorrow was Friday, the day me and Anna used to always spend together. Now, Friday was my day to get fucked up. To try the same shit that she had been doing for so long. I wanted to feel what it was like I wanted to experience what had come between Anna and I. I needed to know.

The next twenty-four hours drug by. The only thing on my mind was doing my first Oxy. I wanted Anna to know that I was doing Oxy too. I wanted her to know how far she had pushed me. I wanted her to understand how much pain she had caused me. I thought if she knew I was doing Oxy, she would understand.

I wasn't going to tell her though. We still hadn't spoken since she told me she had an abortion. She would call me here and there and I would just watch as my phone rang. I didn't have the heart to pick up. I knew she would just drag me back into her world of insanity.

The first day of school, she must have called me about twenty times. She must have been so confused when she didn't see me there. It must have caused her to realize that I was truly done, that we would never be anything. At that point, I was nothing but a ghost to her. I don't know if I haunted her as much as she haunted me though.

Eventually, school ended on Friday. My friend Brian was old enough to drive and had a car so he went with me over to Jake's. We actually beat Jake there. He was still on his way home from school.

We walked into his basement and started bullshitting about what we were going to do that weekend. Him and Mikey were actually getting mushrooms that night and were going to trip. As it turns out, we were all going to be fucked up that night.

The door opened, Jake came in. "Yo!" He threw his backpack down and sat down in front of his computer.

"What's good?"

"I'm so ready to try this out." He reached into one of the drawers in his desk and pulled out a pack of cigarettes. He flipped the pack upside down and out fell a little blue pill. One side of it had an "OC" on it and the other had "80" printed on it.

"I can't believe he finally agreed to sell you one. He's told me no a million times."

"I guess he needed the money."

"I'm glad he did. I've been wanting to try this for a long time."

"So, how do we do this?"

"You have to suck the coating off it first, then crush it up." He placed the pill in his mouth. "The coating is a time release and you don't want that shit.

"Never knew that."

"Yeah, I did some research on it last night."

Jake grabbed his wallet and pulled out a twenty-dollar bill. He placed the pill in the middle of it and then folded the bill in half. He placed two of his fingers along the open edges of the bill. Then, he grabbed his lighter and began to crush the pill into powder.

"Is half a pill enough to get both of us high?"

"Dude, this is will be the highest you've ever been."

A little grin appeared on my face, I had been waiting for this for so long. I watched intensely as he continued to crush the pill. Once he was done, he emptied the powder onto the desk and grabbed a credit card. He used the card to split the powder in half and form two lines.

He looked over at me, "You want to go first?"

"Na man, you got it. Have at it."

"You want to at least pick which line you want?"

I stood up and walked over next to him. I pointed at the line on the right, "That one." They were exactly the same, but he gave me a choice so I took it. Without another word, Jake rolled the bill up and put it just inside his nose. He leaned over the line of powder and began to inhale. As he was inhaling, he traced over the powder with the bill.

He leaned back in his chair and handed me the bill. "Your turn."

I didn't hesitate and did exactly what I had just watched him do seconds before. As soon as I started inhaling, I tasted the chemicals in the back of my throat. It didn't taste very good, but I was doing this for the effect not the taste.

"How long till we feel it?"

"It'll be pretty quick. Snorting it gets it in your system quicker and it breaks down almost immediately since its powder."

"Sweet."

I went outside to smoke a cigarette. I took a seat in the hammock that was just outside of his door and laid back in it. I pulled a cigarette out of my pocket, put it in my mouth and lit it.

I wish Anna could fucking see me now. Look what she had done to me, look at the monster she had created. She had put me in this situation. If I never met her, I wouldn't be here right now. I would still be at my old school, but no, I was here in this hammock waiting for the Oxy to kick in.

I took a drag of my cigarette. I hated her, I hated her so much. I would only feel that hate for a few more minutes before the Oxy kicked in. Once I was high, I wouldn't feel that hate anymore. So, I basked in it for the time being. I let myself be angry. I let myself hate her. I let my emotions flow because I knew they would be cut off soon.

My heart was racing. I wanted to punch a wall. I wanted to call Anna. I wanted to have her back. I wanted to feel her touch again. I wanted to just hear her voice. I wanted to forget everything that happened. I wanted to feel her comfort again.

Then I felt it. It was like someone had slowly draped a warm blanket all around my body. I was completely warm and it gave me the comfort that Anna once did. Slowly, all my emotions faded away into numbness. I felt nothing. Well, that's not true. I felt nothing emotionally. My body felt incredible. I had never experienced anything like this before.

I was in love. The feeling that was just beginning to kick in, was indescribable. There really aren't any words for me to try to convey exactly how it made me feel. Anna had faded from my mind. There was only one more fleeting thought. It was a thank you to her. A thank you for introducing me to heaven. She had lead me here and I was grateful. I had finally found the thing that made me whole again.

That day was the beginning of the end. My demons had finally won the battle. I was attempting to fight, but they were too strong for me and I gave in. I gave in so willingly. In fact, I welcomed it with open arms. My demons had me and they had no intention of letting me go.

My phone was ringing, I was getting a call from Anna. It had been a little while since she had called me. For some reason, I decided to answer. "Hello."

"Hey, it's so nice to hear your voice."

God damn it. This is exactly why I never answer. She knows how to get to me. That immediately opened up all of the scabbed over wounds I had.

"Honestly, I feel the same way. I miss you."

"I miss you too. Why didn't you come back to school?"

Oh shit, this was it. I couldn't tell her the real reason. I couldn't tell her that I was running from her, trying to get as far away as possible. I couldn't do that because a small part of me clung onto the hope that maybe, just maybe, we would find our way back to each other one day. I couldn't burn the bridge even though it would have been the smartest arson ever committed.

"I just thought I would be better off at a new school. People talk so much shit about you and me. They also talk about me getting high. It's like everyone there looks down on me."

That wasn't a lie. Everyone had noticed my struggles with Anna. They saw my pain and they saw me fucked up. I thought I did a good job of hiding it, but I guess I was wrong. There were a few instances where I broke down crying during the school day and people saw. They only saw the outside though, they didn't know the whole story. If only I could tell them, they would understand. I would never do that to Anna though. I couldn't expose her for the monster she was. I loved her too much.

"You left me here though. You always left me when I needed you the most. You don't know how much it hurt me every time I would call you and it would go to your voicemail. I know I fucked up, but I don't think I deserved you to turn your back on me."

"I'm human Anna. I can only handle so much. I'm sorry that I wasn't strong enough for you. I'm sorry that I always let you down. I'm sorry that you and I didn't work out. I'm truly sorry."

"We could have gotten through all of it together."

"How? You started fucking with other people. It wasn't just you and me anymore."

"You know I only loved you though, right?"

The answer to that question was yes. I did know how much she loved me, but I couldn't tell her that. We would go right back to the vicious cycle that I had finally managed to break with her.

"Is this why you called? To beat me up? If this is going to be the whole conversation, I'm hanging up."

"No, I called because I heard you weren't doing good. I just had some questions that I needed answers to first. I called because I still love you and want to see if you're okay."

That was a very deep question. I mean, I was okay when I was high. When I wasn't, I was a train wreck. I still had so many resentments towards her for everything that happened and I missed her. I really fucking missed her. I had started doing OxyContin because of her too. So, no, I was not okay. I was the furthest thing from okay. I broke down. Tears began to well up in my eyes.

"I'm not okay," was all I was able to get out before I completely lost it. Tears were streaming down my face. I was trying to stifle the noises of me crying and compose myself so she wouldn't hear how weak I was.

"What's wrong babe?"

"Everything. Everything that happened between us is completely fucked up and I can't get past it. I can't get it out of my head. Every day I relive the memories and I just want to go back to before everything went to shit. I want you back. I want you in my arms."

"I know how you feel. I still think about it all the time. I'm so sorry for how things unfolded. I really wish we could go back in time."

"Anna, I need to tell you something."

"What's that?"

I could hear the fear in her voice. It was like she knew what I was about to say. "I started doing Oxys."

"Oh Dan. Why? You saw the path they lead me down. Why would you follow me?"

"Because it seemed like my only option. I was so emotionally destroyed that I thought pills were the only answer. I was right."

"It's only temporary. The pain comes back and it comes back even worse. The pills might seem like they are the solution, but it's all a lie. The pills don't help you. Don't you remember that was the reason our relationship started to fall apart?"

"I do." I didn't know what else to say. I knew she was right, but I didn't have a better solution.

"Can you promise me that you won't do them again?"

I wanted to say yes, I wanted it to be that simple. It wasn't. I was falling right into her trap. She had managed to draw me back to her in a brief conversation. She was the drug that I was actually addicted to.

"I'll try."

There were a few moments of silence. Neither of us had anything to say. We were just taking in all the words that had been said. The voices in my head were screaming at me. My heart needed her. I needed her more than ever right now.

"Anna, can I come see you?"

"You want to come over right now?"

"Yeah, I need you. I need to see you and have you in my arms."

"Of course, you can. You know I'm always here for you."

"I love you. I'm going to call Tommy and get a ride there."

"I love you too. Let me know what time you'll be here. I can't wait to see you. I missed you so much."

"Me too. I'll see you soon."

What the fuck had just happened? I had relapsed. I was clean from Anna for about six months. No contact whatsoever. Then, she calls me all of a sudden and ten minutes later, I am on my way to her house. I had told her how much I missed her and needed her. I had completely broken down. All the work I had done to distance myself from her had been erased. I was right back to where I started.

I called Tommy. No answer. I texted him, "Yo, can you take me to Anna's tonight?" A few minutes went by before I got a response. "Sorry man, with my girl. Can't do it tonight."

Fuck, fuck, fuck. I was finally going to see the love of my life. I was going to have her back in my arms, but I had no way of getting there. She was waiting for me. Waiting for my text to let her know I was on my way. I was destroyed. I didn't know what to do.

I called her back. "Hey."

"Are you on your way?"

"No, Tommy can't take me tonight."

"Aw. I was so excited."

"Me too. I fucking need you right now."

"I know babe. We can just stay on the phone for the rest of the night and talk about whatever you want to."

"That will have to do."

We spent the rest of the night on the phone together. We talked about everything that had happened in our lives since we last spoke. I told her all about my new school and new friends. She brought me back up to speed on everything that was going on at my old school. She was still with the same guy, but she had stopped getting high. I mean, she still smoked weed and drank, but there were no more pills or heroin. She was doing good.

I began to question whether or not I had made the right decision to leave my old school. Talking to Anna made everything right in the world. I didn't need drugs when I was with her. She was my drug. She was stronger than any drug I had ever done. She was all I needed and I had left her, left her all alone.

When we finally decided that we both needed to go to sleep, we said our goodbyes and hung up. Then it hit me, I was alone, more alone than I had ever been. I regretted leaving my old school and Anna. I wished that I had made some different decisions. I wished that I could take back certain words I had said, but some things can never be undone.

Anna had always been there for me whenever I needed her. Yet, when she needed me, I was nowhere to be found. She was the strong one, not me. She was able to look past my fucked up exterior and see the real me. After all I had done to her, she still loved me. I had fucked up.

Chapter 10

I woke up the next morning with a feeling of despair. Anna had taken control back over me. I couldn't believe what had happened the night before. She was able to pull me back in so easily. I came running back to her like a lost puppy.

I couldn't let her take control over me again. I had to escape from her again. I had to be stronger. She wasn't the answer. She was the problem. I couldn't let her continue to have an effect on my life. She had only negatively impacted my life. There was nothing positive that came from us being together, only pain.

I was hurting. I needed to escape. I needed to feel nothing. I needed to forget. I needed to get high. I grabbed my phone and hit up my buddy Mark. "Yo, man."

"What's good dude? How was the OC the other night?"

We had begun to refer to OxyContin as OC. "It was fucking awesome man. Jake and I split it and we were wrecked."

"I'm glad you split it. I thought he was going to do the whole thing. I was worried he might overdose."

"Na, it was cool. I'm actually hitting you up to see if I can get another one."

"Um. I'm going to have to see what I can get. I'll let you know in a little bit."

"I appreciate it. Thanks."

Mark wasn't really a dealer. His mom had cancer and was prescribed to every opiate known to man. She was prescribed so much that she never took all of her meds. That meant Mark was able to take some from her and sell them to us.

A little time went by and I was getting anxious. I was worried that Mark wasn't going to be able to get anything. My mind was racing and I needed to slow it down. My phone rang, I got so excited, I thought Mark was getting back to me. I looked at who was calling, it was Anna.

Fuck, I wanted to answer. I wanted to talk to her. I just wanted to hear her voice. I knew I couldn't do it though. I listened as the phone continued to ring. It took everything in me to not answer. Eventually it had stopped. I had done it. I was able to avoid her. I was able to say no.

I couldn't take the waiting game anymore. I called Mark. "Sorry to bother you dude, but are you able to get anything?"

"So, I can't get any OC, but I get methadone."

"What's that?"

"It's a synthetic opiate. It's the same kind of high as OC."

Fuck, I wanted OC. I knew how that made me feel and I needed to feel it again. Since OC wasn't an option, I figured that I might as well give it a shot. "Sure, I'll take it."

"Do some research on it before you take it. I don't want you to die."

Mark was always so concerned about us overdosing, which made sense since he was selling it to us. "You know I will. I don't put shit in my body without looking into it first. I don't want to die either."

"When are you coming by to grab it?"

"I'll probably be over in a half hour. How many do you have and how much?"

"They are ten milligrams per pill and I've got eight of them. Don't take all of them. Four should be more than enough to get you high. They are $5 per pill. So, $40 total."

"Sounds good. I'll text you when I'm five minutes away."

"Meet me at the park."

"Word."

I hung up the phone and called Brian. I needed a ride to get the methadone and I knew he would be down to try them too. I called him and told him that I could get methadone. He was stoked. He had never done it before and wanted to try them too. He was going to hop in the car and come get me.

We went to the park to meet Mark. He was there waiting for us on one of the picnic tables. I walked over to him and made the deal. I went back to the car and hopped in. Brian and I each took four pills. I put mine in my pocket.

"So, what do you have planned for the rest of the day?"

"I've got some shit to do later with my family. I should probably head back home." I lied. I wanted to spend the rest of the day by myself getting high. I didn't want to be around anyone. I just wanted to be alone.

"That's cool man. I'll take you home. I appreciate you hitting me up though. I've always wanted to try methadone."

"For sure, I figured you would be down."

He took me back to my house. When I got home, I went down to the basement, which doubled as my bedroom. A few years ago, my dad and I refinished our basement so I could make it my own sanctuary. I eventually moved my bed down from upstairs and made it into my room. I loved it down there. It was my own space. My parents never bothered me, they let me have that space to myself.

I hopped on my computer and went on the website that I used to look up drugs. The website was great, it gave you all the information about whatever drug you were looking up and it had real user's experiences. It told you how much they took and what they experienced while on the drugs. It allowed me to find out more about whatever drug I was planning on taking.

Today's research was obviously on methadone. I wanted to know how much to take and what to expect. The first time users dosage was anywhere between twenty and eighty milligrams. I had four ten milligram pills, so I had forty milligrams in total. I figured I would do take all of them.

The experiences said that the high came and went in waves. You would feel not fucked up for a little while, then it would hit you hard. It would cycle like this for about twelve hours. The high lasted a long time. Since the high came and went in waves, many users would take more, which was deadly. A lot of people overdose on methadone because they don't realize that they are between waves and take more.

I was satisfied with my research and decided that I would take all four pills. I didn't think that I had any chance of overdosing at that dosage. So, I felt safe taking it.

Most of the experiences were all about users just swallowing the pills. I wanted to snort mine so it would hit me quicker. I took out a twenty-dollar pill and began to crush up one of the pills. These pills were bigger then the OC. They were almost double the size, which meant a lot more powder would be going up my nose. Once the pill was sufficiently pulverized, I dumped the powder on to my coffee table and began to form it into a line.

The line of powder was about two inches long and fairly thick. It was way more powder then I had snorted the first time with the OC. I rolled the twenty up and positioned myself over the line. I began inhaling through my nose, drawing the powder up through the bill and into my nose. It fucking hurt. It felt like I was snorting glass. I stopped about a quarter of the way through the line. I knew there was going to be no way I could finish it. It had hurt so fucking bad. That must be why there were no experiences of people snorting this shit. It's like god damn glass.

I sat there for a minute as I waited for the burning sensation to go away in my nose. I needed to figure out how to take the rest of the pill since it was already crushed up. I had heard about parachuting before. Parachuting is when you crush up a pill and then wrap it in a small piece of a tissue. It makes it so you can swallow it like a pill, but as soon as it enters your stomach, it hits you quicker because it's already in a powder form. So, that was what I did.

I decided that I would just swallow the last three pills since the first one had been so much work. One of the pills would hit me very quickly and the other three would take a little bit more time to kick in. That was fine with me. I had the first pill in me and I was content. I wasn't high yet, but I knew I would be soon. That made everything right in the world. I grabbed the last three pills and placed them in my mouth. I took a drink of water and swallowed them.

It was funny how that as soon as I had taken the pills, all my feelings began to drift away. It was like nothing in the world mattered except for my incoming high. I still was thinking about Anna, but it didn't hurt anymore. Nothing hurt. I was invincible when I had a substance in me. I guess just knowing that I would soon be high was enough to release my stress, to alleviate the pain. My mind knew the drugs were being delivered to my blood stream and my head got quieter. Soon, the drugs would take over and I would no longer be in control.

I turned on the T.V. and put something on to kill time until the high kicked in. I was lost in the show when I started to feel the high wash over me. The first wave was beginning to hit. It was a small wave, but it was something. I was caught in the swell of the wave as it pulled me closer. Then, it rose up over me and came crashing down on top of me. I felt nothing, but warmness. I was enthralled by the sensation. My worries were gone and my mind was at ease. All the pain was gone. The memories were still there, but they no longer caused pain. I was numb.

My phone started ringing. It was Anna. I had ignored her first call because I couldn't bare talking to her. Now that I was high, I could do it. It wouldn't hurt me. I would be okay. "Hello."

"Hey, why didn't you answer earlier."

"Sorry, I was out with my friends. Trying to take my mind off things." Lying had become second nature to me at this point. I couldn't tell her that I didn't want to talk to her earlier. I couldn't tell her that I needed to get some pills in order to feel sane again.

"It's okay. I just wanted to hear your voice."

"Well, I'm glad you called again. I want to say that I'm sorry for last night. I was in a bad way."

"It's okay. I really missed you and seeing you sounded really good to me."

"I know, me too, but I don't think we should see each other anymore." She was silent. She must have been so confused after the conversation we had the night before.

"Why?" I could hear her starting to cry.

"It's just not healthy. I can't handle it. I can't handle not having you all to myself and it just brings back all the bad memories. I'm sorry."

"I guess I understand. I need to go though. Just know that I am always here for you if you need to talk about anything."

"Thanks, the same goes for you."

"Goodbye Dan."

"Goodbye Anna."

Telling that to her was one of the hardest things I ever did in my life. The feeling of wanting someone more than anything in the world, but knowing you can never have them is heart wrenching. I knew I could have her back in the sense that we would talk and hang out, but I would never truly be able to have her. Too much had happened, our history was too fucked up. There was no way to mend the brokenness between us. Even though both of us wanted it so badly, we could never have it.

It turns out that I love methadone. The high was almost as good as OC and it lasted way longer. I had fallen in love with opiates. They were able to take the pain away and make me feel normal for a little while.

Over the next few months my friends and I would try every drug we could get our hands on. We did Percocet, ecstasy, coke, Dilaudid, mushrooms, acid, Xanax, and K pins. We basically were taking anything that we could get our hands on. We wanted to experience everything and see what we liked the best. For me, the opiates still were my favorite. They made me feel a certain sense of numbness and peace that nothing else did.

Then, it happened. Heroin was introduced to me for the second time. The first time, I had seen the first girl I loved all fucked on it. The second time, I would try it for myself. Heroin would become the drug that replaced Anna. Anna had caused a certain high within me that nothing else had come close to until I tried heroin. Heroin was a better drug than Anna.

Chapter 11

Heroin. What does that word mean to you? For me, heroin is despair. It has taken people from me. In more ways than one. It has destroyed families, relationships and friendships. It takes the soul from a person. Leaving nothing but the shell of a human being. Once heroin takes over there is nothing else you think about. Your life revolves around heroin. Heroin is the only thing that matters.

I was soon going to do heroin for the first time. I wouldn't be addicted from the first time. That's not really how it works. Heroin doesn't snatch you from the very beginning, no. It plants its seed and begins to grow slowly over time. Then things happen in your life and that seed is now a sapling, festering in your mind. It reaches out to you and lets you know that it's still there for you. It reminds you how it made you feel the first time and how great it would be to do it again.

The worst part about heroin is that it doesn't just affect the user. It affects everyone around them. Heroin comes in and destroys everything. It rips a life to shreds and leaves you left with nothing. Nothing except the same empty hole that you tried filling with heroin. Except now, the hole is even deeper. It's even harder to climb out of.

Today was just another normal day. Except for one small detail. We were going to do heroin after school. Jake had found somebody that sold it and we had all decided that we wanted to try it. I had told him that I wanted three bags. One bag was about one tenth of a gram of heroin. One bag was enough to get you high. A bag cost about ten dollars. So, heroin was relatively inexpensive.

I wasn't scared at all to try heroin. In fact, I was excited. I wanted to know what it felt like. I wanted to know why Anna had chosen heroin over me. Heroin was going to be the answer to many of my questions. There was no fear about heroin. I wasn't worried about getting addicted. I didn't believe it could happen to me.

I was watching as the clock slowly ticked by throughout the day. My mind wasn't present with me. It was somewhere running through poppy fields, bathing in the sunlight. All I could think about was going to Chris's after school and trying heroin for the first time.

Jake had already picked it up the night before. He had sent us all a text message letting us know. Now, all I had to do was get through the day at school. Then, I would be allowed to escape from reality for a little while. I would be allowed to drown in the effects of the drug and be released from my emotions for a little while.

I was really hoping that heroin was going to be better than anything else I had tried. In fact, I needed it to be. I needed it to explain why Anna had found comfort in heroin instead of in me. I needed to know that heroin provided something that I couldn't. I needed heroin to be the answer.

The day finally came to an end. Brian drove us all back to Chris's house. Once we got there the four of us walked in. It was Mikey, Brian, Chris and myself. Once we were inside we just sat there waiting for Jake. He was on his way from his school, one of his friends was driving him. He would be there in five minutes.

My mind was beginning to race. I was finally about to try heroin. I would find out what heroin was. Till this point, heroin had ruined my life. It had taken Anna from me. It came between us and I was never able to get her back. Heroin had taken her from me forever.

The door opened and Jake walked in. "Yo! What's up guys!" He closed the door behind him and sat down on the couch next to me. He pulled something out of his pocket and put it on the table. It was a small blue object. I leaned over to get a better look. It was actually a bunch of little blue bags held together by a small black rubber band.

"My bad, but I couldn't wait. I did a bag last night."

"So, how was it?"

"You're just going to have to find out for yourselves." He smirked at us. His look said it all. He picked up the bags and distributed them to each of us. He gave me my three bags and I held them in my hand and studied them. They were small blue bags with a little powder in the bottom of them. They had a stamp on the outside of the bag. The stamp was "Lebron 23."

"What's up with the Lebron 23 on the bags?"

"It's called a stamp. That's what the dealers and users use to identify where the heroin is coming from. If it's good, people know where to go get more. Usually, each dealer has their own stamp."

"You know a lot about this shit."

"You have to do your research, so you know what's going on."

"Yeah, I guess that's the safest way to do it."

"Last night I snorted it and it was pretty good, but I heard that if you smoke it, it hits you even quicker. I think we should give it a shot."

"How the fuck do we smoke powder?"

"You can smoke it out of a light bulb or you can smoke it off tin foil with a straw to inhale it. I think tin foil will work better."

"Alright, I'll grab tin foil and a straw."

Chris went into the kitchen to grab what we needed. While he went to go get the supplies, I just stared at the three bags of heroin in my hand. I had what I had been searching for right in front of me finally. I had originally met heroin a little less than a year ago. Now, I was really going to officially meet heroin. I was going to experience it for myself. I was going to know what had taken Anna from me. I was going to understand, hopefully.

Chris came back and handed Jake what he asked for. Jake placed a square of the tin foil on the table and picked up a bag of heroin. He unfolded the bag and poured the powder out onto the middle of the tin foil. The powder was a light brownish color. He picked up the straw and put it in his mouth. He grabbed the tin foil and a lighter.

He lit the lighter and placed it under the tin foil. The powder began to smoke and he inhaled the smoke through the straw. He held it in as long as possible before exhaling. When he exhaled, there was no smoke that came out.

"That's how it's done boys." He passed the tin foil and straw to me. I didn't even hesitate, I took it from him and repeated what I just saw. I saw the smoke begin to rise and started inhaling. The smoke tasted like straight chemicals, but I kind of liked it. I held my breath for as long as possible. I exhaled, no smoke came out. That was it. I had done heroin. Soon I would know.

I passed everything to Chris. I leaned back into the couch and closed my eyes. I was comfortable and I was happy. I wasn't high yet, but I knew it was coming. I knew that soon I would know what heroin really meant. I would know how powerful it was. I just sat there waiting for my first handshake with heroin.

Then, it came over me. It was like a warm blanket was draped over my entire body. It felt like the warmest most gentle embrace I had ever experienced. It overcame my whole body and my head felt foggy. Everything was numb, I couldn't feel anything except that gentle warmness. My mind was drifting away into the fogginess. Then, I felt a tap on my shoulder.

"It's your hit. You feeling it already?"

"Yeah dude, it's amazing."

"I know, right! Take another hit. It gets even better."

That sounded like a great idea. So, I proceeded to take another hit. The chemical taste of the smoke was even more pleasant this time because I knew the feeling that it would provide. I let the chemicals fill my lungs and kept them there until everything was absorbed. I passed the tin foil and sat back again.

That was it. I had done it. I had smoked heroin. I had finally embraced the same warmth that Anna had. I sat there as the high came on even stronger. The euphoria that came over me was like nothing I had ever experienced. There really is no good way to describe it because no words can't do it justice. The closest I can come is that the high was better than life itself. It was like I had found out that heaven did exist. It existed as a powder in the bottom of a small blue bag. All I had to do to get to heaven was consume that powder. I had found my garden of Eden.

We continued to pass around the heroin until we had each used one of our bags so that we had all equally chipped in. There was five of us, so we had smoked a total of five bags. That meant we had all done one bag. We all were just sitting there in silence, embracing this new found feeling that I had fallen in love with immediately.

People always talk about love at first sight and I don't believe in that. I do believe in love at first feel though. That can mean a simple touch, a kiss, sex, or in this case a high. I had fallen hard for heroin. Anna wasn't even in my mind anymore. She was completely fucking erased. It was like someone had taken whiteout to that part of my memory and eliminated every trace of her. The memories of her were replaced with heroin.

I had found solace in the same powder she had. We shared that common bond. Our demons had lead us to the same watering hole where we both decided to drink. We knew the potential consequences of drinking, but we were too thirsty to care. We just needed the water, we needed to consume and we needed to feel something other than how we actually felt.

We spent the next hour enjoying the bliss provided by heroin. We didn't really talk much. There was nothing that needed to be said. The time was spent nodding in out of consciousness, just drifting between sleep and reality.

Chris's parents were going to be home soon and we decided that it was probably best that we weren't there when they got home. We didn't want to be all fucked up on heroin in front of his parents. We all piled into Brian's car and began the trip home to drop every off at their houses.

When I got home, I went in and said hi to my parents quickly before going to my room to play video games. All my friends played video games together at night. That was how we stayed in contact. So, I turned my Xbox on and waited for everyone else to get on.

I was still feeling the high. While I stared at my T.V., my mind began to wander. I was thinking about Anna. Usually when I thought about her, it caused me pain, but right now I was able to think about her and not feel that hurt. I could deal with my memories and not have them haunt me.

I thought about what caused Anna to resort to heroin. My story speaks for itself, I know how I ended up smoking heroin off of tin foil. I know how

I got there, but I didn't know how Anna got there. How did she end up with a needle in her arm? What pain had pushed her off that abyss into the darkness? I wanted to know, but I could never ask her that. I don't think she would tell me.

I spent the next few hours playing video games until I decided I was ready for bed. Before I went to bed, I wanted to get high again. The initial high had worn off and I wanted to feel it again. I wanted to be wrapped in the warm arms of heroin.

I looked up how to smoke out of a light bulb. It turns out it's pretty easy. You just have to clear the electrical components out of the glass bulb, so that you are left with just the glass shell. Then, you just pour the powder in and heat it up.

I did what was described and cleaned out a light bulb. I grabbed one of the bags out of my pocket and poured it into the light bulb. The powder settled at the lowest point. I held the bulb up to my mouth and heated the bulb with my lighter. I began to inhale and once again felt the chemicals hit my taste buds.

I smoked the rest of the powder and laid down in bed. Soon, I felt the warmness come over me, like a warm blanket had been draped across my body. My eyes got heavier as my mind began to dance with sleep.

I woke up the next morning at six. I had about an hour to get ready for school. Before I got ready, I wanted to get high again. I had one bag left and I was going to smoke it. I poured it into the light bulb and repeated the process from the night before.

When I was done smoking, I got in the shower and began my normal routine in the morning. The high hit me while I was in the shower. It was like I had found a long-lost love. It made me whole again. It filled the void that Anna had left in me. It was the answer to all my problems. I didn't want my new love to go away. I wanted to spend every second in her embrace.

That was it. Heroin had become a part of my story. Was it inevitable? No matter what events had taken place in my life, would I have ended up smoking heroin? What if I never met Anna? What if she never tried to kill herself? What if she never shot heroin? What if she never killed our child? Was I destined to do heroin? These are all questions I ponder from time to time.

Over the years, I've come to believe that fate and pre-destination are how the world works. We all have a reason that we are put on this earth and no matter what events occur in our lives, we end up right where we are supposed to be. I do believe our choices affect how we get to these destinations, but our final destination is set in stone. I believe that heroin was inevitable. For whatever reason, I had to experience certain events to become the person that I am. Without these events, I would be somebody else.

Whether you share these beliefs or not is beside the point. I just want you to know how my mind operates. This is how I have coped with the hell that I have endured. Whether I am right or not doesn't matter.

The night that I tried heroin was a turning point. For the last year, my life had been consumed by Anna. Now, it had shifted. I was no longer haunted by her ghost. I had found something else to fill the void and it was heroin. My life shifted that night down a new path. That new path consisted of consuming any drugs that I could get my hands on. It would continue this way until something intervened. There was no way I was putting down the drugs on my own.

The next few months consisted of me taking any drugs that I could get my hands on. I wanted to try everything and experience all the different highs provided by the drugs. I was a garbage can for substances. It didn't matter what it was as long as it provided a mind-altering experience.

The list of drugs included Xanax, k pins, molly, ecstasy, OxyContin, Percocet, acid, DXM, and of course heroin. Although, I had fallen in love with heroin, I hadn't become addicted to it. At this point in my life, I was an addict. I wasn't addicted to one substance. I was addicted to getting high. At fifteen years old, I was an addict.

Chapter 12

Drug habits obviously require drugs and drugs cost money. I was fifteen with no job and no interest of getting a job. My only interest was getting high. This left me with only one option. It was pretty obvious that this would happen at some point. I started selling drugs. I mainly sold weed because weed didn't interest me that much. I was able to sell it and not smoke it all. Sometimes I would sell other drugs, but I would often end up just doing them myself.

Mikey had started to sell a little before I did. I already had a connection for weed and would pick up extra of any other drugs that I did so that I could sell them and get mine for free. This worked out pretty well for me. I was able to get high and not really have to worry about money. I was by no means a king pin drug dealer. I was just a suburban kid attempting to get high.

It's funny how life takes us places we never expected. If you had asked me at the start of my freshmen year where I thought I would be. My answer would have been that I was the starting linebacker on the varsity football team and one of the starting pitchers on the varsity baseball team. I had always loved sports. I would not have believed you if you told me that I would be a drug dealer and an addict. It just doesn't make sense. How can life spin so out of control in a year and a half?

That's the beautiful thing about life. It can change in an instant. It can be for the better or for the worse. Sometimes life gets flipped upside down and it seems like our own shoes don't even fit us, but here we are.

I was sitting in in school suspension. I was there because I had skipped school. When you're in there they just give you all your classwork and expect you to do it throughout the day. I spent a lot of time there and never got any work done. In fact, I was fucked up. I had eaten methadone that morning and was nodding out throughout the day.

My phone vibrated, I pulled it out to check on it.

"Hey! This is the third time I've told you to get off your phone. I'm taking it from you." The teacher moderating said.

"Yeah, no you're not. I'll put it away."

"Excuse me?"

"I'm not giving you my phone."

"I'm going to get the principal if that phone isn't on my desk in the next five seconds."

I rolled my eyes. "Whatever dude." I got up from my seat and placed my phone down on his desk. I went back to my desk and put my head down.

"You can't sleep in here!"

"Fucking commies." I muttered just loud enough for him to hear.

"That's it. You're going to the principal's office."

"Cool, maybe they'll let me sleep in there." When I was on opiates, I was an asshole. Nothing productive ever came out of my mouth. My mouth only got me in trouble. I grabbed my backpack and started heading to the office.

When I got there, I took a seat outside. The principal came out and asked, "Why are you here?"

"I don't know man. Go talk to the dickhead moderating in school suspension."

He didn't reply. He stared at me coldly for a few seconds before going to talk to the moderator. He knew who I was. My school had a bad heroin problem and they kept files on all the kids that were problematic. I have no idea what they did and didn't know, but my friends and I were definitely on their radar.

He came back a few minutes later with my phone in his hand and motioned for me to follow him into his office. I did. I took a seat just in front of his desk.

"So, I heard what happened. I'm going to need you to unlock your phone for me."

"What the fuck does that have to do with me getting sent here?"

"If you don't unlock your phone, I'm going to call the cops."

I sneered, "What are you talking about?"

"I'm only going to repeat myself once, I need you to unlock your phone or I will be calling the cops."

I was usually pretty good about deleting any incriminating text messages. I wasn't worried that they would find anything, but it was the principle of it. I wasn't going to unlock my phone when they had no right to see what was on there.

"I'm going to need an explanation of why you need me to unlock my phone."

"I'll let the cops explain." He began to reach for the phone on his desk.

I didn't want to get the cops involved and I was pretty sure everything was deleted so I gave in. "Fine, I'll unlock it. There's not shit on there anyway."

He extended his hand with the phone in it. He wasn't going to give it to me. He was going to hold it while I entered the passcode. Smart man. If he had given it to me, I was going to walk right out of there. I entered the code.

He began searching through my phone. I assumed he was going through the text messages attempting to find out if I sold drugs. I knew there was nothing in there. He spent the next ten minutes browsing through my phone. Then he stood up and walked out. He took the phone with him.

Fuck, what did he find? There's no way I left any messages about selling on there. I was too paranoid about selling drugs to not delete all my texts. I had no idea what he could have found.

He came back a few minutes later with the super intendent and placed the phone on the desk in front of me. There was a picture on my phone of a few pounds of weed, a scale, baggies and bagged out weed. It was pretty obvious that I was selling from that picture. I couldn't believe how stupid I was. Why did I take that fucking picture? There was absolutely no need. I never even showed anyone that picture. I had to play it cool.

"That's a lot of weed. Pretty cool, right? Why are you showing it to me?"

"You're selling weed."

"Me? No, that's just a picture I found on the internet."

"No, it's not. We have reason to believe that you have been selling and this picture confirms that."

They weren't buying it. I had nothing to say. I wasn't going to own up to it and I wanted to hear what he had to say next. I just kept my mouth shut and stared him in the face.

"If you work with us, we won't kick you out of school. We want to know who you get it from and who you sell to. Also, we want to know who else deals."

I laughed. That was my final straw. They wanted me to rat on my customers and my friends. That wasn't going to happen. "I'm not saying anything."

"Well, if that's the case. We are going to have to expel you from the school. We don't want a drug dealer in our school."

"Go ahead and expel me. I'm still going to sell to the kids that go here. It doesn't matter where I go to school."

"Fine. You can go sit outside. Your father is on his way. We will have a little chat and then he will take you home and I'll never have to see your face again."

I got up and went to sit outside. My dad came in, with a look of pure disappointment on his face. My relationships with my parents had been strained since I switched schools. They didn't like my friends because they knew we all got high together. Now, he found out that his son sells drugs. It had been a rough year for them, but I was so caught up in my addiction that it didn't faze me.

My parents had lost control of me. I came and went as I pleased, there was really nothing that they could do. They didn't even try to punish me anymore, because I never listened. My last real punishment was when they took my phone from me. I had just gone and bought my own. It was at that time that they realized I was a lost cause. They just needed to try to get me through till college. Then, I would be on my own, but for the next three years I would be their problem.

My dad didn't even acknowledge me. He just sat down next to me. The principal came out and asked him to come into his office. They spoke for a few minutes. My dad exited and said, "Let's go."

We walked out to his car in silence. He drove me home in silence and dropped me off at our house in silence. He left me there and went back to work. It was like it didn't even happen. I'm sure he was dealing with the fact that his son was a drug dealer and just had no words for me, which I understood. I was a fuck up, but I was okay with that. I had come to terms with that already.

So, that was it. I had been kicked out of my school high school for selling drugs. My parents didn't know what to do with me. I just kept on getting high and fucking things up. I would end up being placed in an alternative school, which is basically a school for all the kids that get expelled from their high school. I would be placed with all the other fuck ups. They should have just called it "The Fuck Up School."

The relationship with my parents only got worse after I was kicked out. They pretty much wanted nothing to do with me. I mean, I was their son, but they didn't even recognize me. They couldn't wrap their heads around the person I had become. They tried everything they could to straighten me out, but I was too far gone. Nothing they did worked and they had finally given up. There was nothing that they could do for me.

I didn't even care that I had gotten expelled. It just meant yet another new school. I still was going to hang out with the same people, get high and sell drugs. Where I went to school didn't matter to me. All that mattered was getting high.

Anna was only a fleeting memory at this point. My mind had become so dazed with all the drugs I was consuming that she barely even crossed my mind anymore. I had forgotten the reason that I tried drugs in the first place. My memories that had haunted me were replaced with a haze of substances. My mind had been altered through drug abuse.

My new school was just as I expected. It was all the fuck ups that got kicked out of their high school. Most of the other kids were kicked out for reasons like fighting, disobedience, truancy, and possessing drugs. From what I could tell, I was the only one their kicked out for selling drugs.

It was strange because I fit right in with everyone. It was like we all shared the same type of story. Most of us had issues with drugs and we all found solace in each other. It was actually a pretty welcoming feeling that I received at my new school. No one judged, we just got along. It was the first time that I really felt like I fit in at a school. It was probably because we were all troubled kids.

My life outside of school went on like nothing changed. I continued to get high and continued to sell drugs. The alternative school really didn't do anything for me. I was still doing the same old thing. I continued to skip school when I didn't feel like going and even met new customers at the new school.

I was in a downward spiral, freefalling to depths that I never knew existed. No one could catch me. The only question was, where would I crash land? There was no chance I was going to turn things around on my own. This all was taking place during my formative years and my mind had become so warped by drugs. I no longer had emotions, only highs and lows.

Anna had introduced me to my demons, but I was the one who chose to embrace them. They had consumed me. I was now a completely empty individual. I had nothing. The only thing I believed I had was drugs. They were my only friend. My only coping mechanism. My only answer.

Things were about to change though. A helping hand would reach down and pull me out of my descent. It would be another chance. A chance to be a normal teenager. A chance to start over. A chance to live life.

"Dan, please come to the office immediately," chimed over the loud speaker at school. What did I do? I don't ever get in trouble at school. I keep my chin clean here. I got up from my desk and grabbed my backpack and made my way to the office.

I walked into the office and my principal and someone I didn't know were in there. "So, what am I here for."

The stranger spoke, "My name's Mike. I'm your probation officer." He stuck out his hand to shake mine. I was too confused to even acknowledge the fact that he was attempting to shake my hand.

"What do you mean probation officer? I'm not on probation."

"You are now actually. We have been notified of all of your absences and we are placing you on probation for truancy."

"What? You're kidding me right? I didn't even know that you could be put on probation for skipping school."

"Well, you learn something new every day."

"So, what now? What does it even mean being on probation? What do I have to do?"

"First, I'm going to have to ask you to pee in this cup. It's a drug test."

"I don't think I want to do that."

"Why's that?"

"I'm going to come up hot."

"Well, I still need you to pee in the cup."

"Fine." I took the cup and headed to the bathroom. I was so fucked. The weekend before had consisted of smoking weed, eating Xanax, molly, Percocet and drinking. I was about to light this drug test up like a Christmas tree.

I returned to the office with the cup in my hand and placed it on the table. "Here you go."

"Thank you." He placed a lid on the cup. "This is an instant test, we will have the results in a few minutes."

"Okay." I sat in silence, wondering what was going to happen when I came up hot for four different substances. I knew nothing good was about to happen. I had this sinking feeling in my stomach. All I could think about was getting out of this room and getting high. I wanted to escape.

Mike picked up the cup and stared at it for a moment. Then he let out a sigh. "Kid, we have a problem. Well, I should say you have a problem." He paused for a minute, "You have two options. One, I can take you to a detention center. Two, you can go to a rehab."

Holy shit, this was it. The ride was over. The only options I had right now were to get sent away somewhere. I broke down crying. The only words that I could get out of my mouth were, "I need to go to rehab."

That was what I needed to stop me. I needed someone to step in and give me an ultimatum. It was a really shitty ultimatum. It was either go to a detention center and continue to live like a piece of shit or go to rehab and try to straighten my life out. I took the option that seemed better to me. I didn't want to go sit in a detention center for god knows how long. I wanted the easy out. I wanted to go to rehab. I thought it would be a little vacation.

I really had no idea what rehab meant. I had no idea what to expect. I just knew that I had fucked up. I had fucked up big time and I had landed myself in a rehab. I was sixteen years old and about to enter my first rehab.

That afternoon, I got home and my parents were there already. There was also another car at our house. I walked inside. My mom and dad were sitting at the kitchen table with a woman. "Dan, come sit."

"Who are you?"

"Your case has been transferred to me. I'm your new probation officer. My name is Lacy. I'm here to figure out a solution for you. Mike told me that you want to go to rehab."

My mom started crying. I answered, "Yes, that's correct."

"Well, I'm here to go over some things with you and to figure out what facility we can get you into."

"Okay."

"First, I need to ask you some questions about your drug use. I need to know what drugs you have been using. Can you please tell me?"

I looked at her as if she was an alien from another planet. Did she really want me to tell her everything in front of my parents? There was no way I could do that.

She read my reaction perfectly, "Dan, I'm here to help and so are your parents. We just need to know so that we can get you into a facility. At this point, you're not getting in trouble for anything, we just want to get you the help you need."

I took a deep breath and took a seat at the kitchen table. "It would probably be easier to tell you what I haven't done. I pretty much take whatever I can get my hands on."

"I need you to be more specific for me."

"Cough medicine, marijuana, Xanax, k pins, Percocet, ecstasy, mushrooms, acid, Sub Oxone, OxyContin and heroin." When I said heroin, my mom started sobbing. I had never seen my mom like that before. I had put her through a lot over the last two years, but this was more than she could handle. She now knew that her son did heroin.

"Are you addicted to anything?"

"Yeah, drugs."

"I'm serious. I need to know if you are addicted to any substance. Do you need drugs to function on a daily basis?"

"That's a tough question. I don't need drugs, but I do. I don't know what you want me to say to that."

"Do you get physically sick if you don't have any drugs?"

"No?"

"Okay, well I'm going to chat with your parents and we are going to get you into a facility as soon as possible."

"Can I go outside and smoke?"

"Of course."

They were able to get me a bed at an adolescent rehab. I wasn't able to go that day because I had barbiturates in my system. I had to wait three days until I could go because they don't detox people from drugs at the rehab. I had to detox on my own.

There was no detox for me. I wasn't physically addicted to any substances at this point. I was just addicted to getting high. The only detox I had was mental. I had to get through the next three days without any substances. After that, I would go to rehab.

Chapter 13

The three days that I had to wait to go to rehab were literal hell. They were my first three sober days in a long time. That meant I had no mind-altering substances at all. My mind was completely clear, from drugs at least.

My mind was flooded with emotions. I hadn't dealt with emotions in almost a year. All my emotions were masked by drugs. I was in pain. I wasn't physically hurting, but my emotional state was in shambles. I couldn't believe that this is where life had brought me. I was sixteen years old and was about to go to my first rehab. Besides that, all the emotions from Anna flooded back.

The worst memory that came back was of Anna all fucked up on heroin and the abortion. I never dealt with any of the traumatic events with Anna. Now, they were haunting me. I couldn't escape the hell that she had dragged me through. I didn't know how to cope with all the emotions that were flooding my brain.

When the morning finally came to go to rehab, I was ready. I had come to terms with the fact that I needed help. I no longer could help myself and I needed someone else to tell me what to do. I needed someone to have an answer for me. I needed to know how to cope with life without drugs. I needed help.

We pulled up to the building. It was relatively small. It looked like a typical office building. I was scared to death. I didn't know what to expect when I walked in those doors.

"You ready?" My mom asked.

"As ready as I'll ever be."

"I love you. You're going to get through this."

"I sure hope so." I opened the car door and grabbed my bag out of the trunk. The bag contained clothes and a few books that my mom had given me to read. My mom exited the car with me and we started heading for the doors.

When we walked in, it felt like a doctor's office waiting room. I took a seat in one of the chairs and my mom went to talk to the woman at the desk. After a few minutes, my mom walked back over to me.

"You're all set. I guess this is the part where I leave. I love you. I can't wait for you to be better."

"Thanks mom. I love you too." I could tell she was fighting with everything in her to hold back her tears. I can't even imagine how she felt dropping her son off at a rehab. No one ever expects that their child will be the one that gets caught up in drugs, but here we are. This was reality and we all had to deal with it. I gave my mom a hug before she left.

The woman came out from behind her desk. "Hey Dan, my names Tracy. I'm going to show you to your room and then we will get you into group."

I had no idea what that meant, but I didn't care enough to ask questions. I would find out soon enough. "Sounds good."

She motioned for me to follow her. She opened the door out of the reception area and we began walking down a long hallway. There were rooms on either side. It resembled a hallway in a hospital except for the floors were carpeted. We walked about halfway down the hallway before stopping.

"Well, this is it! This will be your room for the time that you're here. I'll give you some time to unpack your things then I will come back to get you."

"Thanks." The room contained three single beds and three dressers. The walls were concrete that was painted white. There was a window that looked outside to a large open field. Two of the beds had sheets on them and the other did not. I figured that would be my bed.

I threw my suitcase onto the bed and began unpacking my clothes into the dresser adjacent to my bed. My mind was relatively quiet. The voices in my head were silent for the first time in a long time. There were no memories of Anna haunting me. There was just peace and calmness. I forgot what that was like.

Once I was unpacked, I sat on the bed and waited for the receptionist to come back for me. I thought about the fact of being sober. The thought of not doing drugs anymore scared me. I had no idea how to deal with life without drugs. For the last two years, my life had been consumed by drugs. I couldn't imagine not getting high or participating in any of the chaos that accompanied doing drugs. I had become attached to all of it. That was my life. Yet, here I was, sitting in a shitty bed in a rehab. I had lost control of my life due to drugs. I was here to try to turn my life around. I was here to attempt to find a new way of life. Would I find the answer?

"Are you ready?" Tracy was back standing in the doorway.

"Yeah, I'm all unpacked."

"Awesome! Let's get you to your first group therapy."

"Wonderful." I hated therapy. My parents had tried taking me to a counselor last year and it didn't go very well. Probably because I wasn't very open with the therapist, but either way it wasn't my favorite thing in the world.

She lead me down the hallway to another room. This room was larger with chairs all around the outside of it. There were about twenty other teenagers in the room and one adult.

"Excuse me guys, this is our newest patient, Dan. Please welcome him after your therapy."

"Welcome Dan. I'm one of your counselors here. My names One Time. Take a seat and we will get going," said the adult in the room.

Once I took my seat, the counselor started speaking. "So, today we are talking about triggers. Triggers are circumstances that make us feel like we want to use. Caleb was telling us about his before Dan got here. Caleb could you continue please?"

"Yeah, so, my biggest trigger is fire. Before I got here, I lit my house on fire. I was all fucked up and nodded out smoking a cigarette. The cigarette caught the couch on fire and the fire destroyed the house. Now, every time I see fire, I want to get high. I want to forget about what happened. I'm struggling with the fact that I burnt down my parents' house. It's all my fault because I decided to shoot heroin though. It's fucked up that even though heroin caused my issue, I want to go back to it."

It turns out I was sitting next to Caleb. Caleb looked about eighteen years old. He had longer hair and looked a little disheveled. He resembled a punk rocker almost. He spoke in a very quiet and monotone voice. He seemed like he really was haunted by the memory of the fire.

When he spoke, I realized that I was right where I needed to be. I was surrounded by other people my age that escaped their memories by getting high. Caleb was dealing with the same demons I was. Although they were a little different, we both coped in the same manner. I felt that I was home. Maybe I actually would be able to get my life together here.

"Thanks Caleb. I find that identifying your triggers helps you to recognize them and prepare you for when they occur. You need to have a plan on how to cope with your triggers so that you don't relapse. Dan, would you mind going next?"

For real? I just got here and they already want me to speak? "Um, sure. I'm not really sure what makes me want to get high. I know that I started getting high because my ex did heroin and because of some other things that happened with her."

"So, would you say that your ex is a trigger?"

"Yeah, I guess."

"Thanks Dan."

That first day in rehab, something clicked. I realized that I really was a drug addict. I realized that rehab was exactly where I needed to be. Life had happened and I turned to drugs. Through heavy drug use, I became an addict. The definition of an addict is one exhibiting a compulsive, chronic, physiological or psychological need for a habit-forming substance, behavior, or activity. It turns out that I fit that definition. I was an addict.

The thing about addiction is that it is a chronic disease. That means that I will deal with it until the day I die. Addiction isn't cured. It doesn't just go away. Addiction will be something that I battle every day for the rest of my life. Some days will be easier than others, but as long as I'm alive, I will be an addict. I will either be in active addiction or I will be recovering. Recovering means that I am sober. Active addiction means that I am abusing a substance. In order for me to stay sober, I have to not take any mind-altering substances. This includes drinking. At sixteen years old, that is a lot to except.

The rest of that day was spent talking with the other kids in the rehab. We swapped stories of how we ended up there and what drugs we did. We also talked about selling drugs and hooking up with chicks. We basically exchanged all of our best memories of getting high. We didn't talk about the shitty parts of being addicts.

It turned out that most of the kids in there how no desire to stay sober. Most of them ended up there because of legal issues, just like myself. There only intentions were to get through rehab to keep themselves out of detention centers. There were only a people there who actually wanted to stay sober. These were the people that I gravitated to.

After the first group therapy, I decided that I wanted to be sober. I didn't want to get high anymore. I wanted to learn to cope with life without using. I knew where using took me. It took me to dark places that I wish I had never visited. Now, I had the choice to never visit those places again. I no longer had any drugs in my system. This meant that if I ended up getting high it was because I made a conscious decision to pick up a drink or drug.

I finally had control back. It was now up to me if I wanted to use again. I was once again behind the steering wheel. I had the power to make the decision to not use anymore. I never wanted to get high again. I wanted a clean start.

Since I had been kicked out of my last school. I made the decision that I wanted to go back to the school that I started high school at. They actually were closing the school this year to merge with another catholic school. They had built a new high school and that was where I wanted to go.

The reason that I wanted to switch back was because I didn't want to go to alternative school anymore. I didn't want to hang out with my same friends. I needed to get away from them if I was going to stay sober. If I went back to them, I would get high again. I thought that the new school would give me the best chance at sobriety.

The only issue with this was that Anna would be in my life again. I would have to see her at school. I would have to see the guy that she was with. I would have to deal with all of these emotions sober. I believed that I could handle all of that. I was actually excited to have Anna in my life in a healthy manner. I didn't want her in a romantic way. I just wanted to be friends with her. I was actually excited to see her again after so long. We hadn't even spoken in about six months.

I still loved Anna at that point and I still do to this day. There are a few people that I have crossed paths with that I will always love. I gave them a part of my heart that they will have forever. That's how I love. I give away pieces of myself to people that I believe deserve it, whether they actually do or not is another story. Anna is one of these people.

The turmoil she put me through shaped me into the person that I am today and I thank her for that. I thank her for everything we went through together because they were all lessons. Lessons I wish I never had to learn, but every lesson is valuable. It proves that we can make it through situations that no human being should ever have to experience.

Life is a rollercoaster and while I was in rehab I began the slow climb back to the precipice.

I learned things about myself and thought that I could go back to the real world and survive as a normal human being without drugs or alcohol. I no longer wanted to use substances to cope with life, but sometimes the valleys of the rollercoaster get dark. They can become pitch black with no escape. How would I handle those moments?

I started to spend a lot of time with Caleb. He was like me, an old soul who carried more pain than any one person should. We were able to burden each other with our own pain to alleviate the weight on our own shoulders. We shared all of our stories, right down to the ones that I never planned to tell anyone, but there was something about him that really sparked my interest. He had shot heroin.

Caleb had been an intravenous heroin user for the past year. He was addicted in every sense of the word. He could not start the day without heroin. If he tried, he would be sick. Sick to the point of puking, aching and not being able to sit still. He described withdrawal as the worst sickness you could ever imagine. The worst part is that you know how to make yourself better, but the medicine only hurts you more.

I didn't really care about withdrawal, I wanted to know what shooting heroin was like. Sure, I had snorted and smoked heroin, but I never used a needle. I was deathly afraid of needles and the thought of sticking one in my own arm scared the shit out of me. Yet, I wanted to know what it was like. I wanted to know what Anna had felt. I had only scraped the surface of heroin. Anna had dove headfirst into its depths. I wanted Caleb to tell me what it was like. I needed to know.

"So, what's it like?"

"What's what like?"

"Shooting heroin."

"Don't do it. It will ruin your life and everything around you. It will bring a new hell into your life that you can't even use words to describe."

"I don't want to do it. I just want to know what it's like. I don't ever plan on getting high again. So, the closest I'll ever get to experiencing it is you telling me what it's like."

"Well, close your eyes. I don't know if you believe in an afterlife, but let's imagine you do. Picture what heaven is for you. I can't tell you what that is, but just picture whatever it is that makes you happiest in life."

I didn't believe in heaven, but the first thing that came into my head was Anna. She was sitting on the beach staring out into the water. She was just watching as the waves broke onto the sand. She looked beautiful. She had the glow around her that drew me to her from the moment I saw her. I began to approach her and as I got closer, I noticed a child playing in the sand next to her. It was Ava. My heart was full. I walked over and sat right between my two girls. There were no words spoken, just smiles. Our facial expressions said the words that our mouths never could. This was my happy place, my heaven.

"So, are you in your heaven?"

I kept my eyes closed. "Yeah, I'm there."

"How do you feel?"

"I feel whole. I no longer feel the pain or emptiness. I have everything I need and I am truly happy. My heart no longer hurts and everything is absolutely perfect."

"That's what shooting heroin feels like. It's better than anything else on this earth. It's a taste of what heaven is like. Once I felt it the first time, I never wanted to feel any other way. Yet, it fades and you have to do it again. You have to do more and more to bring you back to the heaven you once felt. It'll never really be the same as the first time, but it's close enough. The rush you get from shooting heroin is like injecting yourself with that feeling of heaven."

"I guess I understand why people get addicted to it."

"No, only the people who have shot heroin can understand that. You can imagine what it's like, but hopefully you'll never try it for yourself."

"Yeah, you're right. I don't want to use anymore. I don't want to give into that false hope of drugs."

I lied. I really wanted to shoot heroin now. I wanted to find out for myself what heaven felt like. I decided that that if I ever did relapse, I would shoot heroin. I didn't plan on relapsing, but if I did, I had to feel it for myself.

Rehab was going pretty smoothly. I got along with everyone there for the most part. I had even made a few friends. The real friends that I had found in rehab were reading and writing. Reading provided me with an outlet. It allowed me to escape to another reality, just like drugs had. It allowed me to dive into someone else's shoes and experience life through their eyes. Reading was my new escape. Writing had become my way of expressing my emotions. It allowed me to put all my feeling on to paper and get them out of myself.

I wasn't always good at talking to people about how I felt, but with writing I was able to talk to the universe. I didn't actually have to talk, I just put my words on paper and my emotions were made real by doing that. It was an outlet that I had never tried before and I really liked it. I began keep track of all my days in a journal. I kept track of what happened that day and how I felt. I planned to write a book when I got out of rehab and I wanted to keep a journal to make that happen. I planned to put all my journal entries into the book.

Sorry for the disappointment, but those journals are long gone. I wish I still had them to insert excerpts from my sixteen-year-old mind into this story, but they disappeared with time. I wasn't ready to write my book after that rehab trip. I still had more of my story that I hadn't lived yet.

My reading and writing kept me occupied through the down parts of the day. We actually had quite a bit of down time between activities. They tried to keep us pretty active, but there are twenty-four hours in a day and you can only spend so many of them in therapy.

The day started early with breakfast at seven. Afterwards, we would do our schoolwork until lunch time. It was close to the end of the year, so we all had to continue our school in order to finish the year. After lunch, we got to spend an hour outside. Then we would have therapy sessions until dinner. Therapy sessions had a wide range of variation. They ranged from talking about our history of drug abuse to our plans of the future. After dinner, we would have one more group meeting then we were allowed to have downtime until ten. Then, we would do our chores and get ready for bed. The next day, we would do it all over again.

After the first week, I was ready to go home. I missed my parents. I had never been away from them for this long before. I wanted to go back to the real world and give this being sober thing a try. I didn't think I needed to spend any more time in rehab, but my parents and probation officer disagreed. I had to complete my stay there, which entailed a total of thirty days. The thirty days was only if I didn't get in any trouble, so I had to stay on my best behavior.

The days slowly ticked by as I grew more accustomed to life without drugs. Believe it or not, life felt normal, or as normal as it can when you're in a rehab. I felt like I was actually living a life again. I was doing exceptionally well in school. I had always been smart, but my drug use detracted from my school work. In fact, I never did any school work when I was getting high. It felt good to be back to myself again. I was also making friends, something that I didn't enjoy while I was getting high. I had my close friends and I didn't want to talk to anyone outside of them. My world was slowly going back to what it used to be. I couldn't change the events that had happened to me, but I could change the person I was. I would always be a drug addict, but I could choose to be a recovering addict.

The best part was that I could think and talk about Anna without feeling all the pain I used to associate with her. It was like my wounds had finally began to heal. The drugs had just masked the pain, but now I was dealing with the pain and it was beginning to heal. I still thought about the terrible memories with her, but I also thought about the reasons I fell in love with her. I began to accept that she was a drug addict too and we are both human, which means were flawed. None of us are perfect and we all make mistakes. It's how we handle those mistakes that define us. For too long, I let drugs define me. I let my demons have control. I wanted that control back and I was taking it.

I had now made it through three weeks and I finally had the end in sight. That day, we got a new patient. His name was Alex and we had both gone to the same alternative school. When I saw his face in rehab, something clicked in me. I no longer wanted to be associated with the people I surrounded myself with. I didn't want to end up in another rehab and seeing someone that I knew. I didn't want to associate myself with people that end up in rehabs. I couldn't believe that I had ended up in an alternative school, but that's what happens to people like me. We slowly progress down a road that ends with jails, institutions and death.

I had avoided jail by going to an institution. If I kept going down the path I was, I would end up back here or dead. There were no other possible outcomes for a drug addict. There's no happy endings when drugs are involved. All the possible endings are tragedies. No one is able to do heroin and get through life unscathed.

If there was any doubt in my mind before, when I saw Alex's face, I knew I never wanted to get high again. I wanted to change my story. I wanted to be somebody in life. I no longer wanted drugs to control my actions. I wanted a chance at life.

I made it through that last week of rehab. I came out a new man or a new teenager I should say. I was still very young and very impressionable. I didn't know what life had in store for me, but I knew that I didn't want it to involve drugs. When I walked out of that rehab, I truly believed that I would never use again.

I believed that I made the best decisions I could under the circumstances to give me the best shot at living life without drugs. I believed that going to another "new" school would be my best option. It would get me away from my old group of friends and put me around people that I had known for a large part of my life. I thought my elementary school friends and new friends would allow me to build a new life. It didn't bother me that I would have to go to the same school as Anna.

I was actually hopeful that Anna and I could be friends. I still loved her. I didn't love her in a romantic manner, but I loved her as a human being. I was able to look past all of the mistakes she had made and accept her for who she was. I was able to see her humanity, which allowed me to love her flaws and all.

I was excited to rebuild my relationship with my parents and get my life back on track. I wanted to get my grades back up and get into a good college. I wanted to play sports again. I wanted to be the person I was before drugs had come into my life.

Chapter 14

I got out of rehab at the end of June. Summer was already in full swing for all of my friends, but this summer was going to be different for me. My parents had grounded me for the rest of the summer, which I was okay with. The old me would have disregarded the punishment and did as I pleased, but I wanted to change. I believed listening to my parents was the first step in changing.

Although I was grounded, I was allowed to get a job and go to narcotics anonymous meetings. These meeting were supposed to help recovering addicts stay sober. I didn't know if it would work, but I figured that it was the best chance I had at staying sober.

The first thing I did when I got home was start applying for jobs. I didn't want to spend my summer sitting in my parent's basement, so I figured work would be the best way to get out of the house. I began applying to any place that was hiring near me. I really didn't care what the job was. I really just needed something to get me busy and mind occupied.

The first night that I was home, I went to my first ever narcotics anonymous meeting. I had no idea what to expect. In fact, I was a little nervous. I didn't know why, but I was very apprehensive of walking into the building.

My dad and I were on our way to take me to a meeting. It was right around the corner from my grandma's house. My dad was going to drop me off and go spend some time with her. The meeting was only an hour long, so he wouldn't have to wait that long for me.

We pulled up to a church. Apparently, that's where most of these meetings take place. I hesitated before I got out of the car. It was another moment where reality hit me and it hit me hard. I was about to walk into a room full of recovering drug addicts. The reason I was going there was because I'm a recovering drug addict too. That's a tough realization at my age. I let reality sink in for a few minutes before I got out of the car.

I finally got out and walked towards the entrance of the church. There were a few people out front smoking cigarettes and talking with each other. As I approached, someone greeted me. He was an older guy with white hair, but dressed like he was in his twenties. It seemed like he was stuck in believing he was still young, maybe that was a good thing.

"Hey! How's it going? My name's Ed."

"I'm Dan. Nice to meet you." I shook his hand. I grabbed my cigarettes out of my pocket and lit one.

"So, what brings you here?"

"I just got out of rehab today and I'm trying to stay sober. So, here we are."

"Well, we are glad to have you! Once you're done your cigarette come on inside and get your chair. We'll save it for you."

I didn't know what that meant at the time, but it's something that now resonates with me. It is a privilege to have a seat in meetings. It means that your sober. My seat signifies that I'm no longer using drugs and have found a new way of life.

We can give up our seat whenever we want though. We give it up by going back to drugs. We give up our chance of a new life and turn back to our old ways. Yet, narcotics anonymous will save that seat for us. We will always have a seat in the room if we make it back.

"Thank you." I said. Ed seemed really nice, but I usually don't get along very well with overly nice people. Then again, I was trying to change my old ways. Maybe I needed to give him a chance.

I puffed on my cigarette as more people walked into the church. The people that walked in seemed normal in every sense of the word. There were old people, young people, men and women. If you saw these people out in the world, you would never guess that they were drug addicts. The only reason I knew they were was because they were walking into a meeting.

I was taken back a little bit. I never realized that drug addicts were just like you and me. These people at the meeting were normal people whose lives had been encompassed with drugs. Something had happened and drugs had taken control over them, but they were fighting to stay sober just like I was.

I finished my cigarette and went inside. The room was large and there was a large circle of chairs with one chair in the center of it. There were about thirty chairs circling the center chair. I was curious who the center chair was for. It was a little strange seeing that chair in the center of the circle.

Most of the seats were filled, but I found an empty one and took a seat. The meeting was just about to start. One of the people in the circle began talking. He read from a paper that talked about what narcotics anonymous was. Then he said, "The chair in the center of the room represents the addict that didn't make it back to this room and the addict that will find their way here."

That hit me hard. I realized that not every addict is lucky enough to find their way into one of these chairs. I was blessed to have been sent to rehab and been instructed to attend these meetings. I very well could have been that addict that never made it to this room. I still could be that addict that loses his way.

The meeting was surprisingly interesting. People talked about how they were dealing with life sober and how they were able to manage a life without drugs. It was amazing to me to see all these people who had gotten off drugs and were able to live a normal life again. I was excited to be one of these people.

That first meeting I went to made me feel at home. I was surrounded by people just like me dealing with the same issue. Although how we go there varied, we were all there for the same reason. Those people gave me hope that it was possible to live life without drugs.

I believed that room would be my new answer. My old answer was drugs. They solved my problems. Now I believed that those rooms would be my solution. I thought that they could save me from my demons, that they could relinquish my pain.

I got a job working as a dishwasher in a kitchen. It wasn't much, but it was something to keep me busy through the summer. I actually enjoyed the job and the people I worked with. I got along with them well and they gave me other jobs besides just washing dishes.

I now had a job and meetings to fill up my time. Life was good as far as I cared. I was off drugs and moving forward with my life. Soon enough, school would start and I would really get a new chance. I was excited for the summer to be over and to start again at another new school.

I made some friends close to my age at the meeting I went to and my parents started letting me go out with them. I guess they thought that if I was hanging out with sober people that I was making smart decisions with my life. They began to trust me again and allow me to do things that were safe for my sobriety.

I had fun with my new friends. I hadn't had fun in a long time. My life had consisted of just getting high. Now, we went bowling, paintballing and out to eat. We shared stories and talked about sports. We were living what I considered a normal life and I was truly enjoying it. My life had yet again changed course drastically. The only difference this time was that it had changed for the better.

The rest of that summer went by quickly. The school year was now upon me and facing Anna again was inevitable. I didn't know when I would see her, but I knew I would have to. I started getting those damn butterflies in my stomach when I thought about seeing her again. I missed her, I missed her a lot. It was going to be nice to see her face again. I just hoped that it had the same glow that it did that night I fell in love with her.

The first day at school was going well. I had seen friends that I hadn't seen since my freshmen year. They were surprised to see me, but they were glad to have me back. I was happy to see familiar faces along with new ones. My school had merged with another catholic school, so I only knew about half the people in my grade.

I had been placed in mostly honors classes because that's what I was in when I had gone to the old school. Even though I had done poorly in my sophomore year, they understood my situation and gave me a chance.

The only problem I had with my class schedule was that they had placed me in Spanish four, which meant I had been taking Spanish for three years prior. I had only taken one year of Spanish and I had done extremely bad. There must have been some mistake by the school that I would have to work out.

In the meantime, I had to go to the class and talk to the teacher. I walked to the classroom and went it. As soon as I entered, I saw her face. Our eyes had locked immediately and we shared a smile. It was like we had both seen a long-lost friend. She had the same glow about her that she had the night we met. She looked just as beautiful as I remembered.

I took a seat as the teacher walked into the room. "Don't get too comfortable everyone. I will be assigning the class seats. Please stand up around the outside of the classroom while I give everyone their new seat."

We all got up and lined ourselves along the wall of the classroom. She began reading names off her list and the students filled in their assigned seats. The rows of the classroom were slowly filling up and neither mine or Anna's name had been called.

It was down to the last row and both of us were still standing against the wall. Finally, my name was called. I walked over to my seat. It was three desks back from the front of the classroom. As I walked over to my seat, Anna's name was called next.

What were the chances of that? I knew I was going to have to see her, but now I'm going to have to talk to her too. I didn't know if I was ready for that. It really was great to see her, but talking to her was a whole other animal. I began thinking of what to say. I really didn't have any words for her.

She sat down in the desk behind me. I felt a hand run through my hair. "I like your hair like this." She said. I had let my hair grow out since I had left freshmen year. In fact, I hadn't had a haircut since the last time I saw Anna. My hair was now touching my collar. I used to get a very short buzz cut all the time.

I turned around as she said that. She was smiling at me. It was the same smile I saw when she walked into my classroom in freshmen year. It was the same smile I had fallen in love with. "Thanks, you look…" I paused as I just stared into her eyes. "Perfect."

"Am I going to have to change seats already?" The teacher said sharply.

"No, it won't happen again." I replied.

I no longer wanted to change my class. I wanted to stay in this class with Anna. I wanted to be as close to her as I possibly could. I wanted to have her back in my life. I wasn't going to talk to my teacher after class and try to get my class changed. I was going to make this work.

I don't really believe in god, but I do believe in something. Whatever I believe in was playing some cruel fucking joke by putting Anna and I in the same class and having her sit right behind me. This was about the last thing I needed at that time.

The bell rang and the class was over. I stood up and Anna grabbed my arm. "Can we walk together to class?"

"Sure, just like old times."

We exited the classroom and started walking. "I had heard you came back."

"Yeah, I'm sure I'm the talk of the school once again."

"So, why are you back?"

"Well, I got kicked out of the public school and sent to an alternative school. Then I ended up in a rehab. I thought coming back was the best option I had." The look in her face contained so much pain. She knew what the word rehab entailed. She knew I had gone down a dark road and it cut her to her core.

"I'm sorry. Are you okay now?"

"Yeah, I've been sober for three months now. Everything is okay."

"I'm so proud of you."

I wanted to ask her about her using, but I decided it was better if I didn't. Sometimes it's better to not ask questions you don't want to hear the answer to. She looked like she was doing well and I just hoped that she had escaped her demons too.

"Thank you. Well, I need to get to my next class. It was really good to see you."

"You too." She leaned in to hug me. I wrapped my arms around her for the first time in a little over a year. Her embrace brought back all the good memories of her. I couldn't let myself fall into that delusion though. I knew that her and I could never be anything. Too much shit had happened between us and things could never be like they were. I had to remember that. Seeing her gave me that false hope that drugs used to. I couldn't do it.

Instead of going to my next class, I walked to the principal's office. I needed to get my schedule changed so that I was in the correct class. I couldn't make it through that class because I didn't know any Spanish.

I was running away from Anna once again. I thought that I wanted her in my life as a friend, but I couldn't handle that. It wouldn't be healthy for me. If we were friends, we would end up back in the same cycle of love and despise for one another. I had to walk away for my own sanity.

This was a weird time in my life. I was attempting to learn how to live without drugs and with Anna. I wanted her more than anything in this world, but I knew I could never have her. At least not in the way I once did. There was too much pain still to ever have a normal relationship with her. Yet, I couldn't get her out of my head. I didn't know if going to the same school as here was the right decision. At the same time though, going to a different school didn't work either. I was just going to have to deal with the hand I was dealt.

I was transferred out of the Spanish class that I had with Anna and put in one that was my level. I got a text from Anna asking if everything was okay the first day I wasn't there. I told her the situation and that was the extent of our conversation. I really wanted to call her and spend the rest of the night on the phone, but I knew I couldn't. My mental state was too important to me and I couldn't let her affect it.

My sobriety was going well. I really didn't even think about doing drugs or drinking. I was actually happy living a life without drugs. I was slowly growing into a new person and I had found a new freedom now that my demons no longer controlled me. I wanted to continue to keep my head on my shoulders and not give into temptations, which included the temptation of talking to Anna.

Anna was with a new guy, but that didn't bother me. The other men in her life never bothered me because I knew they would never have her like I had her. Even though we didn't talk anymore, I still knew she loved me. That smile she gave me when we saw each other in Spanish class said it all. Yet, she fucked with my mental state too much. I knew that if I relapsed it would because of a situation with her. I needed to do everything in my power to keep her at arm's distance.

I'll never forget what Caleb said about going through withdrawal from heroin. You know what will make you feel better when you're sick, but the medicine hurts you even more. My relationship with Anna was just like heroin. She was my slice of heaven. When I was away from her, I felt physically and emotionally sick. Yet, having her in my life would only hurt me more.

The difference between love and drugs is that once the drugs are out of your system, you don't need them anymore. You're free. Love never lets you go. No matter how hard I tried to forget about Anna, she was always in the back of my mind. I had to learn how to live with her occupying space in my head.

Heroin is a dangerous drug, but love is the most dangerous drug in the world. Love was what lead me to heroin. That's why I believe that love is more dangerous. Love can lead people to do things that they thought they were never capable of.

Chapter 15

It was the Saturday before Halloween and one of my friends was having a huge Halloween party. Everyone from school was going to be there. That included myself and Anna.

This was going to be my first party ever sober. It was going to be a little weird not getting fucked up at a party since I used to always be the most fucked up person at the party. Yet, things were different now. That wasn't me anymore. I was a new person and I planned to continue living a sober life.

My dad took me and my best friend Mark to the party. Mark's dad was going to take us home afterwards. The party was about forty minutes away so we had a long car ride there. My dad bullshitted with us about school and what was going on in our lives.

When we got there, there were already quite a few people there. The party was outside. We could see about fifty people there already. There was a bonfire and that's where most of the people were.

We hopped out of the car and headed over to the crowd. We went around and said what's up to everyone. I introduced myself to anyone that I didn't know. Eventually I found a minute to myself and took a seat by the fire. I stared into the fire and let my mind drift away for a few seconds.

I was brought back to reality when I felt someone sit down next to me. It was Anna. Why was it always Anna?

"Hey!" She had a water bottle in her hand. I knew there was no water in it. The liquid in the bottle was vodka. I could tell she was drunk already.

"Hey, nice to see you."

"You too!" She wrapped her arms around me. I didn't really know what to say. I wanted to tell her how much I missed her and that I wanted her back in my life, but I couldn't. So, she did it for me.

"I've missed you so much. I'm so glad you're back at school. It's nice just to see your face from time to time."

Fuck, why did she always do this to me? What did I do to deserve this? All I wanted to do was keep her out of my life, but she kept pulling me back in. She kept telling me exactly what I wanted to hear and dragging me back in. It was a cat and mouse game and I was the mouse.

"Honestly, I've missed you too. I think about you all the time." I did it. I said the words that I never should have said. I opened my fucking mouth and allowed my heart to get the best of me. My brain knew I fucked up, but my heart was happy.

"Why do you never text or call me then? I am always happy to hear from you."

"Because I'm scared Anna. I'm scared of what I did in the past and I don't want to do it again."

She must have just remembered that I was sober and that she was drinking right next to me.

"Shit, I'm sorry that I'm drinking. I don't want to bother you with it."

"No, it's fine. You drinking doesn't bother me. I never even liked drinking, you know that."

"I just wanted to make sure. Can I ask you something?"

"Anything."

"Do you still love me?"

Fuck, my heart was screaming yes. Yet, my mind was telling me to walk away from the conversation. My heart has always been bigger than my brain though. "I do."

"Can I hear you say it? I miss hearing it."

"Anna, I love you. I have since the moment I met you and I will love you to till the day I die."

I saw a tear roll down her cheek. I knew she missed me just as I missed her. At that moment, I realized she knew just as I did that her and I would never work together. "I love you too Dan. Can we just sit here for a little while?"

I smiled. "Of course."

She moved a little closer and rested her head on my shoulder. I'm not sure how long we sat there for. It could have been a life time and it still wouldn't have been enough. We both gazed at the fire, not saying a word. We just enjoyed each other's presence. We had been apart for so long that it was nice to have her next to me once again.

Life had taken its course on the both of us. I didn't know what had occurred in her life since the abortion, but I knew she was still filled with pain, just like me. We were two lost souls who for a minute found comfort in each other. Although that comfort wouldn't last forever, it was everything to feel it in that moment.

Our time together was broken when someone called out my name. "Yo Dan! Come over here!"

"Mark's calling me. I'm going to go see what's going on."

"Okay, it was really nice seeing you."

"You too." I smiled. She leaned in and kissed my cheek.

I got up to go see what was going on. Mark and a few other guys were over by the pool. I walked over to them.

"Dude, Mike's going to jump off the roof of the shed into the pool! You want to do it too?"

"Fuck no. I'll jump in, but I'm not jumping off the roof."

"Pussy." Mike said as he stripped down and climbed up on to the shed. As soon as he was up there he jumped off and into the pool. The rest of us preceded to jump off the edge into the pool.

We got out quickly because it was about thirty degrees outside and ran over to the fire. Anna wasn't there anymore. We all sat down by the fire and watched as the flames flickered and the heat from the fire warmed us back up.

The party went on for few more hours, Mark's dad was about to be there to pick us up. I wanted to find Anna and say goodbye to her. She still wasn't at the fire.

"Yo Jake, you know where Anna's at?"

A girl sitting next to Jake responded, "She's somewhere with Tom."

Fuck, that was not what I wanted to hear. After the conversation I had with her, how could she do that? How could she walk away from me and go hook up with another guy? Other guys didn't bother me normally, but that cut me to the core. I was angry, upset, and I didn't know what to do. My mind was racing. I wanted to get high. I didn't want to feel this bullshit anymore. How the fuck did I let her do this shit to me again? How could I be so dumb?

I made my decision right there that I was going to get high tonight. I didn't know what I was going to get high on, but I was going to get fucked up. I wanted to escape and I was going to. I didn't care about being sober anymore. All I wanted was to not feel this pain.

After six months of being sober and mending my wounds, Anna had torn open all of those wounds. She had drawn me back in and had me hook, line, and sinker. I loved her so much and yet I couldn't have her. I couldn't deal with it, I needed to get high. I needed to forget.

Mark's dad picked us up and I didn't say a word the whole ride home. I was busy texting people to see if I could get some drugs. Nobody had anything until I hit up a kid I went to alternative school with. All he had was Vicodin, which is a shitty painkiller. I told him I would take as many as he had. He had ten, which was enough to really fuck me up. I had only done Vicodin once before because it's not very strong, but I knew ten of them would have me where I wanted to me. I told him to be at my house in a half hour.

Mark's dad dropped me off and I thanked him for the ride. I only had to wait another ten minutes until Paul would be there with my drugs. I went inside and said hello to my parents. Then, I went out back to smoke a few cigarettes until my drugs arrived. My parents knew I smoked and they didn't really care. They figured me smoking cigarettes was nothing compared to what I used to do, so they allowed it. Little did they know that I was about to relapse.

Paul got there right on time. He texted me to come out. I walked around my house to the front and he was parked at the house next door. I walked over to the car.

"You're a life saver man. I really needed these tonight."

"Yeah man. No problem."

"What do I owe you?"

"Forty."

Forty dollars for ten Vicodin was bullshit. I could get four bags of heroin for that price, but it was the only thing I could get tonight so I was happy to pay the price. I just needed something to take the pain away.

"Here you go." I reached into the window and handed him the money and he gave me the pills.

"I'll talk to you later." I walked back around my house and went back inside. I told my parents that I was going to bed for the night and headed into the basement.

I went down into the basement and took a seat at my desk. I reached into my pocket and pulled out the plastic bag containing my pills. I opened the bag and poured them onto my desk. The pills were rather large and since there were ten of them, I couldn't snort all of them. I decided that I would parachute half of them and swallow the rest. They were seven and half milligrams each, which meant I would be taking seventy-five milligrams in total. I was going to be right where I wanted to be.

Parachuting pills is when you break the pills into powder and place the powder in tissue paper. This allows you to swallow the powder and when it reaches your stomach the powder is absorbed quicker because your stomach doesn't have to break down the powder.

I proceeded to break up five of the pills into powder. It broke out into way too much powder to put into one parachute. So, I made two parachutes. I stared at the powder wrapped in tissue paper for a few minutes.

Here I was yet again. Anna had pushed me past my limit and I had resorted to the only thing that always loved me no matter what. Anna had told me she loved me and then went and hooked up with some guy. Anna always found a way to hurt me. The drugs never did. Maybe this was what I was meant to be, a drug addict.

Without thinking anymore, I picked up the first parachute and placed it in my mouth. I took a sip of water and swallowed. I repeated the process for the next one. After that, I swallowed the leftover five pills. Now, it was time to wait.

I had just thrown out my six months of sobriety. I was no longer sober, I was back on drugs. It didn't bother me that I was no longer sober. In fact, I felt at peace with myself. I felt like drugs were my only friend and we had finally been reunited. I had missed everything about getting high. Even though it landed me in rehab, I didn't care. Drugs were my solution to dealing with life. Anna found solace in other men, I found it in a substance. We all have our demons, mine presented themselves in a powder.

Here we are yet again. This was my relapse. I had found my way back to drugs or maybe drugs found its way back to me. I yet again let Anna control me to the point that I needed to find an escape. The only escape I knew was drugs. I always thought that maybe if I found a new girl that maybe it would replace Anna.

I had talked to other girls since Anna, but none of them were good enough. They weren't Anna. No woman could replace her at that time in my life. The only way that I could fill the void that she had left in me was through drugs. Drugs made me whole again.

I didn't know it at the time, but that relapse would lead me to places I never imagined going. I knew that Anna no longer had a place in my life and that was what caused me to get high. For a long time, I wanted her in my life to some extent. I wanted to save what we once had. Yet, I finally realized that she was gone forever. I would never her back and that hurt. The only way I knew how to fix that pain was to get high.

When a drug addict uses, the consequences don't matter. We don't care about what will happen. We only care about getting high. We know that there are consequences of using, but we will deal with those as they happen. The only thing that matters is where are next high will come from.

Chapter 16

Anna was gone and so was I. I had finally let Anna go. I knew her and I were nothing but memories. As for me, I was back on drugs. I was right back to where I was before I went to rehab. As soon I relapsed, there was only one thing on my mind, shooting heroin.

I didn't care about anything else. Everything that I had worked for the last six months had gone out the window. My sobriety was gone and so was everything that came with it. I no longer cared about school, my sober friends, or anything at all. The only thing that mattered to me now was my next high.

I woke up the next day after I relapsed. There was only one thing on my mind, heroin. I wanted to know what it was like to shoot heroin and I was going to do that today. I was going to experience what it was like for myself. I was anxious. I needed to do it.

I hit Jake up to see if he could get any heroin. He told me that he had a guy who could get it whenever. I told him that I wanted a bundle. A bundle is twelve bags of heroin. He told me that we would let me know once he had it.

Now that I knew I was going to get heroin, I needed to get syringes. In Pennsylvania, any pharmacy will sell you syringes. All I had to was go to the pharmacy and buy them. I did some research online to find out exactly what to ask for. I found out that a common diabetic needle is 29 gauge, 1cc, and a half inch. This just refers to the different sizes of needles. I figured this would be a good one to buy just in case they asked me what is was for I could tell them that I was diabetic.

The rest of the day I spent watching football waiting for Jake to get back to me. My mind wasn't present though. My mind was focused on heroin and experiencing what Anna had. I was excited to be only hours away from experiencing my first real heroin high.

Around six that night, Jake finally got back to me. He told me that he had it and I could come grab it whenever I wanted to. I told him that I would borrow my parents car and be over in a little bit.

I went upstairs to talk to my parents. "Hey mom, can I borrow the car to go to a meeting?" I was already lying to my parents and it hadn't even been a full twenty-four hours since I relapsed.

"Of course, the keys are on the table."

"Thanks mom. I should be home around eight thirty."

"Have fun. Be safe."

I grabbed the keys and hurried out the door. My first stop was going to be at Jake's to pick up the heroin. Then I would go to the pharmacy to get needles. Jake only lived about five minutes away and I had to kill sometime since I told my mom that I was going to a meeting. I planned to spend some time at Jake's so I didn't raise any suspicions with my parents.

I got to Jake's and walked into his basement door. He was sitting at his computer as usual. "What's up, man?" I shook his hand.

"Yo dude? What happened? You haven't been getting high and then all of a sudden you want a bundle. Everything okay?"

"Take a guess."

"It's because of Anna, isn't it?"

"How'd you know?" I said sarcastically.

"Man, when are you finally going to let that chick go? She has been nothing but trouble since you met her."

"I don't know how to explain it, but she just has this fucking power over me. No matter what I do, she is in my head. All of the shit that happened with her fucking haunts me and the only thing that helps is drugs."

"Love's fucked up."

"I couldn't have said it any better myself. I think I'm finally getting past her though. I've accepted the fact that her and I are never going to work. That's why I got high last night."

"So, what happened last night?"

"I went to Halloween party that she was at. She came over to me and we talked for a little while. Then, she went and hooked up with some dude that I don't know."

"What a fucking bitch."

"Yeah that shit hurt, but it finally made me realize that her and I were never going to work. I cope with my feelings by getting high and she copes through other guys. We're both fucked up."

"Yeah you are." He laughed.

"So, how much do I owe you?"

"One hundred. I'm giving it to you for what I get it for. I'm not making anything off you."

"You never have, so I didn't think this would be anything different."

"I just didn't want you to think I'm ripping you off."

"Never man." I reached into my pocket and pulled out my money. I counted out a hundred dollars and placed it on Jake's desk. He reached into a drawer and grabbed something. He handed me the bundle. I immediately slid it into my pocket.

"Be careful with all that. You can overdose if you do all that shit too quickly."

"You know me man. I always am safe with taking drugs."

"I know, I just wouldn't feel right if I didn't say it."

"I appreciate it. I plan to make it last for a while. I'm actually going to shoot it."

"Hold up, why didn't you tell me? I've been wanting to shoot it for a while."

"I honestly didn't think about it until now."

"You got needles with you?"

"Na, I'm going to get them when I leave here."

"You want to come back here once you got them?"

"I kind of want to do it when I'm home so that I don't go home all fucked up. My parents still think I'm sober."

"That makes sense. Well, let me know how it goes."

"Definitely. Do you mind if I chill here for a little bit? I told my parents I was going to a meeting, so I have to kill some time."

"Yeah man. You know you're always welcome here. Let's go smoke."

We walked outside and sat down in the chairs just outside of his basement. It was dark out, but the moon illuminated the skyline. It was a beautiful fall night. It was cold, but I enjoyed this time of year.

I lit my cigarette and took a drag. I now felt content. I had had my heroin in my pocket and I was going to shoot heroin tonight. I was finally going to dance with the demon that had tormented my life for so long. I was going to let that demon fill my veins and take control of my body. I was going to succumb to its power.

There was no fear, only hope. Hope that heroin could provide me the relief that I so desperately needed. That it would explain why Anna chose heroin over me. I was about to feel the same high that she loved so much. I would have the same track marks that she made me feel. I would be the same as her, a heroin user.

"Are you scared to die?" Jake asked. I was taken back by the question. I had drifted off in my own thoughts and didn't fully realize what he said.

"Huh?"

"Are you scared to die?"

"Um, I don't know. I've thought about death a lot. I mean, you know I wanted to kill myself not that long ago."

"I don't mean to be an ass hole when I ask this, but why didn't you?"

That was a tough question. The easy answer would be that I was afraid to die, but that wasn't the truth. "Honestly, I believe that I was put here for a purpose. I don't think that my purpose was to kill myself at fifteen years old. I don't know what my purpose is, but since I'm still here I know that I was supposed to survive that. Also, us surviving the accident was another sign. We all should have died that night, but here we are. There is a bigger purpose for all of us. That's why I keep fighting."

"That makes sense. I've been thinking about it a lot and death doesn't really scare me either. I've accepted the fact that I'm going to die. I just want to live as much as I can until that day comes. Yet, the only time I feel alive is when I'm high. I don't know how we ended up here man."

"I understand completely. I spend too much time thinking about why we've gone through everything that we have. My only answer is that for some reason we need to experience this. We need these moments to shape us into the people we'll become."

"I like how you think. I like that you believe in some greater purpose. I don't know if I do, but I'm going to try to start thinking that way."

After that heavy conversation, we sat in silence for a little bit, then we bullshitted about sports and video games for a while. We smoked a few more cigarettes and enjoyed the company of each other. I checked my phone and it was time for me to leave. It was almost eight and I still had to go to the pharmacy. I said goodbye to Jake and got in the car.

The pharmacy was only about ten minutes away. I started driving and put on music to keep my mind occupied. When I got there, I sat in the car for a few minutes prepping myself to go inside to buy needles. I practiced what I was going to say to the pharmacist.

Finally, I stepped out of the car and went inside. I walked to the pharmacy and waited a minute before someone came over to help me.

"Hello, what can I do for you?"

"I need a ten pack of syringes. Can I get the 29 gauge, 1cc, and half inch syringes please?"

The pharmacist looked at me for what seemed like forever. I'm not sure what she was thinking about, but I assumed she knew. I assumed she knew that I was going to use them to shoot heroin. It seemed like I had broken her heart. She legally had to sell them to me, but it seemed like every part of her being wanted to say no. Finally, she walked back to get what I had asked for.

She came back to the register. "That will be $2.97."

"Here you go." I handed her the money. She placed the syringes in a bag and gave me my change.

I took the bag and hurried back to my car. I placed the bag in my sweatshirt pocket and went and got back in my car. I immediately turned the car on and rushed home. I had the needles and heroin in my pocket. There was only a short amount of time left before I would shoot that heroin. I was completely relieved.

When I got home, my parents were sitting in the living room. "Hey guys."

"How was your meeting?"

"It was good." I was always brief with my parents.

"Glad to hear it."

"I'm going to head down stairs. Goodnight guys."

"Goodnight. We love you."

"I love you too."

I walked down the stairs and took a seat on the couch. I pulled the bag of needles out and placed them next to me. I also grabbed the bundle out of my pocket and placed it next to the needles. I took one needle out of the bag and one bag of heroin out of the bundle. I took the rest of the heroin and needles and put them in my stash spot. It was a spot in one of the closets in my basement where I hid all my drugs and drug paraphernalia.

I put everything else away because I only wanted to do one bag that night. I put everything away right away so that I didn't nod out and leave anything out for my parents to find.

After everything was stashed away, I took a seat back on the couch. I placed the needle and bag of heroin on the coffee table. There was a bottle of water still on the table from the night before. I had everything that I needed to shoot heroin.

I twisted off the water bottle cap and placed it upside down on the table. I opened the bag of heroin and poured it into the bottle cap. Then I picked up the needle and took the cap that protected the needle off of it. I placed the needle into the water bottle and drew up enough water to fill half the needle. I shot the water into the bottle cap with the heroin. Then I proceeded to stir the heroin into the water until it was a dark murky brown.

The myth about heroin is that users always use a spoon and a lighter to heat the heroin. The reality is that no heroin user that shoots powder heroin does that. All you do is waste heroin by burning it.

I stared at the murky brown water for a minute. There was still no fear, only excitement. I was finally about to feel what heroin was like. I grabbed my pack of cigarettes and broke the filter off of one of them. I took a small piece of cotton from it and placed it in the murky solution. I picked the needle up and placed the tip on the piece of cotton that had now absorbed some of the solution. I drew the plunger back and sucked up all of the heroin water.

Now, all I had to do was find a vein. I had always been terrified of needles, but right now I didn't care. I knew this needle meant that I was going to get high and that made everything tolerable. I held out my left arm and saw a vein in the crook of my arm. I positioned the needle towards my body and placed the tip just on the skin over the vein. I slowly slid it in and drew back the plunger slightly. Blood filled the needle. That meant I had hit a vein. Now, all I had to was push down on the plunger and I would feel that heroin high.

I slowly depressed the plunger and watched as the solution disappeared into my arm. Before the solution was completely in my vein, I felt the heroin coming on. It was like nothing I had felt before. Sure, I had snorted and smoked heroin, but this was different. I didn't know that it was possible for a human being to feel like this. I was overcome with a sense of warmth and relief. My head felt like it was floating above my body and all my pain was gone. All of the nightmares that haunted me were forgotten. I had found heaven and met god. That's the best way to describe it. Heroin was now my god and I never wanted to feel any other way. I never wanted to leave this new-found heaven.

I finished depressing the plunger into my arm and pulled the needle out of my vein. I hid all of the gear under the couch in case my parents came down. I sat back on the couch and closed my eyes. I let the high wash over me and consume every part of my being.

There is no way to put into words exactly how the high feels. In fact, I forget to some extent. I don't remember exactly how it felt. I mean I haven't shot heroin in over six years now. I remember that I loved it. I remember that I never wanted to feel any other way, but I can't tell you exactly how it felt. I know that I had found my new love though.

I wouldn't say I was addicted from that first shot because I didn't start using consistently right away. You don't become a heroin addict overnight. It's one of those things that progresses without you even realizing it and then all of a sudden you need heroin. I wasn't there yet.

I had found what I had been looking for since the time Anna made me feel her track marks and tell me that she used heroin. I felt that since that night this was my destiny. I was fated to shoot heroin. This was exactly where I was supposed to be. I was supposed to stick a needle in my arm to get high. Everything that had happened with Anna had lead me to this moment.

Chapter 17

Everything had come full circle. It had been almost two years since I had met heroin for the first time. We had met that night at Anna's house when she came down from upstairs and had me feel her track marks. Now, I had shot heroin. I had finally gotten my answer as to why Anna had chosen heroin over me. The answer was simple, yet hard to understand. You could only understand if you tried heroin. Once you try heroin, heroin makes sense. Yet, if you've never done it, it is the most perplexing issue.

Heroin is the closest you will ever get to heaven while here on earth. You walk among the angels and you feel at home. It's almost as if you've actually died and are experiencing the next life. Heroin takes away all of your pain and your problems. Nothing else matters when you're high. That heaven doesn't last very long though, it slowly fades away. Then, you're suddenly back in this shitty world with all your problems and you just want to go back to that little slice of heaven that you found. So, you go and get more heroin and you do it all again. Eventually, you will do whatever it takes to get back to that little slice of heaven.

Anna had discovered her own part of heaven and that was why I faded away as a priority. I wasn't as important as heroin. My feelings and our relationship came second. Heroin always comes first. I couldn't understand that until I tried heroin. When I felt it enter my veins, everything was explained, it all made sense. I could forgive Anna for letting heroin be her priority. I could get past that now. I could finally start moving on.

After six months of being sober, my life had changed course completely after a brief twenty-four hours. I had relapsed and shot heroin. Now, I wasn't sober anymore. Everything that I had accomplished while sober was thrown out the window, that shit didn't matter anymore. The only thing that mattered was getting my next high.

That's how sobriety works, it's like a light switch. When you're sober, the lights are on and everything is clear. You have found your way out of the dark and started to make progress in your life. Drugs seem like a thing of the past and you slowly start to recover. Then you decide to turn the lights out. You decide that drugs are the answer once again and your world goes dark. You are now living in the darkness, it's a completely different world. Everything that you accomplished with the lights on can no longer be found. In fact, you don't care to find it. The only thing you want to find is your next high.

I was now back in the dark. I had to keep up the façade to my parents that I was still sober though. I didn't want them to know that I was back on drugs. I had caused them a copious amount of pain the last time I was using and I didn't want to do that again. I was going to try to do everything I could to keep up the act that I was sober.

Therefore, I didn't go back to hanging out with my old friends. I continued spending time with people from my new school. If I went back to my old friends, my parents would know what was going on.

The next few months consisted of being binging on heroin and then not doing any for a little while. I was a very sporadic user. I would use for a week straight and then lay off it for two weeks. There was no rhyme or reason to it. It wasn't because I didn't want to become addicted, being addicted never even crossed my mind. I just didn't have access to heroin all the time. So, when I did I would buy one or two bundles and then I would shoot heroin until I didn't have anymore. When I didn't have any more I would just drink, do other pills and smoke weed.

Anna was no longer a concern to me. All the pain that she caused me still existed. It was just masked by all the substances that I was putting into my body. I hadn't healed from it, I had only put a Band-Aid on my wounds. Yet, the Band-Aid felt amazing. I never wanted to take the Band-Aid off.

Anna and I hadn't spoken since the Halloween party. She had texted me a few times to check in on me, but I had ignored the texts. I felt that she didn't deserve a response. She had caused me so much pain and led me right to where I was at. She didn't deserve to know what I was doing. She had lost that privilege a long time ago. Although, I had continued to play into her games, I was really done with her now. I really wanted to throw it in her face that I was shooting heroin, but that wouldn't alleviate any of my pain. It would only cause her pain. I wanted to be a bigger person than that. Therefore, I wallowed in my pain by myself.

I'm sure that Anna heard about what I was doing through the grapevine. Our school was small and everyone talked. I'm sure my drug use had gotten to her at some point. Somehow, that made me feel better. I know it had to hurt her to hear it from someone else. I really didn't want to hurt her, but I found comfort in the fact that she didn't learn about my usage first hand. She was close to the end of the line in the fucked up game of whisper down the line.

At this point, I wasn't even chasing any girls. High school is usually a time when guys try to go after as many girls as possible, but I didn't see the allure in it. Sex wasn't even on my mind. That was because heroin was far better than sex for me. Nothing compared to heroin and that's why heroin was my top priority.

Once I relapsed, the rest of my junior year was pretty much a big blur. This was the first year that the chaos of Anna had finally dissipated. She was no longer a factor in my life. The only factor in my life was drugs. I stayed in a drug induced state as much as I could. This was limited due to me not having a job, so once again I went back to selling drugs.

Once again, I was no kingpin, but I did have the best connections at our school. Anything that I could sell, I did. It was mostly just weed, but whenever I could get extra Percocet, coke, molly, or anything else really, I did. I would sell what I could and do the rest. I didn't make any money as a drug dealer. All I was able to accomplish was that I supported my own habit. Selling drugs allowed me to get high as much as I wanted to.

I had to lay low though because I was still on probation, I didn't get piss tested anymore because my probation officer believed that I was still sober and so did my parents. I had somehow managed to relapse and keep it completely hidden from my parents. I had successfully kept up the charade that everything was okay in my world. When in reality, I was spiraling out of control.

I had spiraled out of control before, but this time was different. This time I had fallen in love. Heroin had its hold on me and it had no intention of letting go. There really was no end in sight. I didn't want to ever stop doing heroin, but I knew that I couldn't go on forever doing heroin.

That spring, I tried to occupy some of my time by trying out for the baseball team. Baseball had been my favorite sport since I was a little kid, but I hadn't played since my freshmen year. I knew that if I made the team, I wouldn't have as much time to get high. I was okay with that. Getting high is complete chaos and I wanted some time away from the chaos.

I was never able to throw the same way after I had injured my shoulder. My arm just didn't have the same range of motion anymore. I guess that's what happens when you break a collar bone. I still went to try outs though and gave it everything I had, that's just how I am. Whatever I choose to do, I give it everything I have. I leave nothing left. Yet, I came up short. I didn't make the team. I wasn't really upset about it though. I had given it my all and that wasn't enough. I knew that the rest of the year was just going to consist of drugs and partying. Baseball wasn't going to save me.

The thing about drugs is that it wears you down over time. The mental and physical toll that it takes on your body can be debilitating. You believe that the drugs are your medicine. That they are the only way to make you feel okay, but in reality, you are slowly killing yourself. I was getting worn down and close to the end of the school year, I knew I had to stop.

I didn't want to be sober, I just wanted to stop doing hard drugs. I wanted to go back to just smoking weed and drinking. Everything else needed to be eliminated from my life. How I planned to do that was by getting a job to fill up my time. So, I took a class to become a lifeguard before the summer started. When I started the class, I stopped doing hard drugs and it worked. I was able to just smoke weed and drink. I finished the class and had a summer job lifeguarding lined up.

That summer was one of the best summers of my life. I was working forty hours a week and partying my ass off the rest of the time. I managed to keep it to drinking and smoking though. I'm not sure how I did it, but I did. I was still selling drugs though. I was actually able to start saving some money since I wasn't spending as much on getting fucked up anymore.

Once I had a little money saved, my mom agreed to sell me her old car. It wasn't much, but it was something to get me around and give me the freedom of having a car. My parents had fully given me their trust again, even though they had no idea what was really going on. For the first time in a while, I believed that I was actually happy. It seemed like everything was going right for me for once.

Although I had cut the hard drugs out, drinking had now become a problem. I never really liked drinking before, but now it had become my only outlet so I learned to like it. The problem was that I was a black out drinker. I would be blacked out about a half hour after I started drinking every time. I would wake up the next day and have absolutely no recollection of the previous night's events. I would remember bits and pieces, but beyond that I had no idea.

Addiction is a fascinating disease. It manifests itself in multiples ways. Although I had eliminated drugs from my habit, I had created a new one. There was no way for me to escape myself. If I left behind one substance, I just found another. Now, my habit was drinking. At the time, I didn't think it was a bad thing. I just told myself, well at least I'm not shooting heroin anymore.

My junior year was the first year that no major traumatic events happened. I don't consider shooting heroin a traumatic event because I chose to do that. I made the conscious decision to stick a needle in my arm. Shooting heroin was the biggest life event that happened. It was a paramount event because it led me to wear I ended up, but was it traumatic? No.

I was still in a very dark place, but it wasn't because of Anna anymore. It was all due to my drug use. I had now been abusing mind altering substances for two full years. Those two years are critical developmental years and I had crammed my brain full of drugs. I wasn't mentally developing anymore. My mental development had ceased the night Anna tried to kill herself. From that point on, I didn't know how to cope with life. The only coping mechanism I knew was getting high, so that was what I did. I had no idea how to live life without getting high.

Although I had been sober for a brief period, once I started using again everything I learned about coping was once again thrown out the window. Any healing that taken place during my sobriety had been nullified. I was now just a completely broken human being.

Chapter 18

I had made it to my senior year. I was finally almost done high school. My last year of high school would be the worst year of my life. That year would take me to the darkest places I had ever ventured. Places so dark that no human being should ever be present. I would go as far as calling these places hell. The reason that I no longer fear death is because I experienced hell already. I don't know what awaits us after this life, but I know it can't be worse than what I have already experienced.

My life up until this point had been far from perfect, but this year would be even worse. I look back on this time in my life and I have no idea how I made it out the other side. My only explanation is that for some reason I need to be alive. There is something greater than me that still needed me here in this life. I truly believe that's the only reason that I am still here. The odds were stacked against me and I should have died.

Anna had been creeping back into my mind lately. It wasn't because I wanted to be with her. There were just questions that I needed answered and things I needed to say. I guess you could say it was the closure that I really needed from her. I really had moved on, but I thought if I could have one more talk with her that maybe she would stop haunting me.

It turns out I was wrong. There are some things that happen to us in life that we never get over. We have to carry the weight of that burden for the rest of our lives. We don't move past it. We have to learn to live with it. Anna was one of those things. I still think about everything that happened with her today. I wonder how she's doing and if she was able to find happiness.

I had to learn to carry the weight of her introducing me to heroin, trying to kill herself, and killing our child. At first, I didn't carry that weight, I masked the memories with drugs. When I finally got sober for good, I learned to carry that weight and cope with the memories. Everyone learns to carry their own weight in different manners. There is no right or wrong way to do it, we all have our own way.

I decided that I would reach out to Anna so that we could have the conversation that I thought I needed. So, I texted her and asked her if we could meet at the mall that we used to spend time together at. It was the middle point between where we both lived. We set up to meet that coming Saturday at two in the afternoon.

Saturday arrived and I got in the car to go meet her. For the first time ever, there was no butterflies in my stomach on my way to see her. I knew that meant that I really was over her. I wasn't going to talk to her to try to get her back. I was going to talk to someone that once held all of my heart. I was going to get my closure. I'm not sure why she agreed to meet me as we hadn't talked in almost a year. I guess she still had love for me as well and wanted to do whatever she could for me.

I pulled into the parking lot and parked my car. I got out and walked into the mall. Anna and I were going to meet at the coffee shop in the mall. I started walking in the direction of the coffee shop. As I got closer, I saw Anna walking in from the other direction. I smiled at her and got that perfect smile she had in return.

"Hey."

"Hey, how are you?"

"I'm doing good, I think. How about yourself?"

"I'm doing really good. So, what did you want to meet about?"

Where to start? "There's so much that happened between us and I just wanted to talk to you about some of it. Over the last few years I've really struggled with everything that happened and I thought maybe this would help provide me with some closure."

"Yeah, we've been through so much since we met. I know you've really struggled since everything happened. I've struggled too. I don't say that to make you feel bad, I just want you to know that nothing that happened with us was easy for me. It took a toll on me as well."

"I know that. I'm just hoping I can get some answers to some of the questions I have."

"So, where do you want to start?"

"Well, the thing that fucked me up the most was the abortion. I want to know why you didn't tell me about it?"

Anna let out a sigh. She had to know this question was coming. "Well, I knew how you would react and honestly I never planned on telling you. The pain just became too much for me to carry on my own and I felt that I had to tell you. I knew that you were adopted and you never would have been okay with me doing it, but I believed it was the best decision for both of us. I was doing drugs and we both were only fifteen. We had no right to bring Ava into the world."

"Honestly, I hated you for that. I never thought I would forgive you. There's not a day that goes by that I don't think about her. Yet, I've had a lot of time to think about it and I agree with the decision you made. I don't agree with you not telling me before hand, but I believe you made the right decision. I just wish you would have told me before you did it so we could have talked about it and we both could have made the decision. I wish I could have been there for you through it all."

"Thank you for that. I think about her everyday too. I just know that we have our own guardian angel watching over both of us for the rest of our live and that makes me smile."

I smiled. I found comfort in that thought often as well. "I know we do and we're lucky to have that. That's something we'll share forever."

"Now, I have a question for you."

"Go for it."

"I think I know the answer, but why did you switch schools after freshmen year?"

"I believed that you and I were never going to be anything and I thought that if I stayed at school we would have stayed in the toxic cycle we had been in. I loved you so much and I thought getting away from you was the best option for both of us."

"I don't know what would have happened had you stayed. I think you and I still had a chance."

"Anna, you fucked me up bad that year. I got into drugs and thought about killing myself more than I'd like to admit. We were completely toxic. I don't think we ever would have worked out. You had other guys in your life."

"Well, I guess we'll never know." She paused. "I dealt with everything that happened through men. I need you to know that you always had my heart. They never had me like you did. They were just how I coped. I was trying to stop doing drugs and talking to guys helped keep my mind off heroin."

"I know that. I mean, I know the other guys were just filling the void that you had. I didn't know you stopped doing drugs, but I figured because you look healthy now. I really just don't know that I could have mentally handled going back to the same school as you."

"But you did. You came back last year."

"Yeah, enough time had passed and I was sober. I thought that I could deal with seeing you and it turns out I was right to some extent."

"I was so happy to see you that first day of school. You looked like you were doing so well and you looked happy. It was like you were back to the person I met way back at my New Year's Eve party."

"I was doing good. That's why I believed that coming to this school was the best option. Things got really bad at my last school."

"I hate to ask this, but are you still doing good?"

I knew this question was coming. I'm sure she had heard rumors, but I didn't know if I should tell her or not. I didn't want to cause her any unnecessary pain, but I didn't want to lie to her either. "I'm sure you've heard rumors. I don't want to tell you anything that's going to hurt you, but I'll tell you if you want."

She looked at me for a minute. I could see in her eyes that her heart was breaking. She knew what I was going through. "Yeah, I would like to hear it from you and find out what's true or not."

"I relapsed last year. I started shooting heroin and my life spun out of control again. I'm doing better now though. I'm only drinking and smoking. I couldn't keep doing hard drugs."

"Why'd you relapse?"

Fuck, I hoped she wouldn't ask that. There was no way that I was going to tell her that I relapsed after the Halloween party. I couldn't do that to her. It would kill her. Even after all the pain she caused me, I didn't want to do anything to hurt her. I wasn't going to lie to her, but I wasn't going to tell her the whole truth either. "I just ended up in a bad place mentally and ended up taking some pills. I didn't want to feel how I was feeling anymore and I decided that getting high would make me feel better."

"Well, I'm glad you're doing better now. I don't do pills or heroin anymore. I haven't done any of that stuff since sophomore year. I just smoke and drink now too."

"I'm proud of you. I really am."

"Thank you."

We sat there in silence for a little bit. We were both just taking in everything that had been said. I wanted to talk to her about the abortion and if she was still doing drugs. Everything I wanted to talk about had been said. I had gotten what I came for and was okay with everything that had been said. It was a lot, but I needed that.

She finally broke the silence, "Can we be friends after this?"

"Yeah, I think I'm finally ready for that."

"Good, I still want you in my life. I still love you even though you and I will never be anything again."

"I still love you too and I always will. You and Ava will always hold a spot in my heart even if we're not meant to be."

She smiled at me. "Thank you. Is there anything else you want to talk about?"

I thought for a second. I wanted to ask about the overdoses and her trying to kill herself. I wanted to know whether or not all of them were real or just cries for attention. Yet, I didn't really need an answer. Some things are better left unsaid and I think that fell into this category. "No, we talked about everything I wanted to. Thank you for coming to talk."

"Of course." She stood up and so did I. I gave her a hug. I kept my arms wrapped around her for what seemed like an eternity. I didn't want to let go, but I knew I had to. I knew that when I let go of her, I was letting go of everything that happened between us. I wanted to hang onto all of that for as long as I could. Finally, I let go and let go of her. It took me almost three years to let go of her, but I finally knew I had to do so completely.

"I'll see you around."

"Text me sometime."

"I will." We walked away from each other. I had taken a few steps and then turned around. I watched as she walked away. I was watching the person who had been the biggest influence on my life walk away. She was the reason why I was standing where I was and I was watching her walk out of my life. This was the end of our chapter.

She turned around and saw me looking at her. She gave me that smile that I had fallen in love with and kept walking. I was okay with her walking away. I was okay with ending this chapter of my life. I had finally gotten the closure I needed and could move on with my life. I was truly okay with everything.

I had finally closed the door on Anna. What that meant was that I had left everything that had happened with her in the past. There was no way for me to change what had happened and I had to be able to accept it and move on with my life. I couldn't let her control me anymore. She had run my life since we met that fateful night.

So much had happened in the three years that I knew her. My life had changed dramatically in that same time frame. My life had become unrecognizable to me, but I believe that everything happened for a reason. For some unknown reason,

I had to be burdened with all the events that took place. I needed these events to happen to me to shape me into the person that I would become.

For a long time, I blamed Anna for my addiction. Now, I look back and thank her for everything that happened. Without her, I wouldn't be the person I am today. Today, I am happy with who I became. All my life experiences have shaped who I am and I will be forever grateful to Anna for that.

Anna and I met in the middle of October of my freshmen year. I thought that after our talk I would be able to start moving forward instead of just treading water. I couldn't have been more wrong. My life was about to be flipped upside down once again. Death would knock at the door and I would answer. I would look death in the face and he would take someone who didn't deserve to die.

It was the first day back at school after Thanksgiving break. I had just taken my seat in my literature class when I heard my phone vibrate in my backpack. I didn't bother looking at. The class started and we were working on a group project so we broke off into our groups.

I went to my group and started talking with everyone. Then the one girls in my group asked me, "Did you hear that someone died at Perkiomen Valley?"

That was the high school that I went to my sophomore year and was kicked out of. "No, I didn't. Do you know who it was?" I was worried.

Most of my friends there did drugs and it very well could have been any of them.

"I think his name was F."

My heart sank. Tyler was one of my friends that I hung out with all the time my sophomore year. I immediately reached into my backpack to check my phone. There was a text from Jake. It said, "Tyler's dead."

My head started spinning and I had no idea what to do. I needed to call some of my friends and find out what the fuck was going on. I raised my hand. "May I use the bathroom?"

"No, you have to wait a little bit. Someone is already in there."

"I'm going to the bathroom." I got up from my seat and began to walk out.

"You'll be going to the principals after."

One of my friends chimed in. "Please let him go. Something really messed up just happened."

I heard the teacher say, "You're excused," as I was already walking out the door.

I went out into the hallway and called Mikey immediately. It went straight to voicemail. I called another one of my friends to see what was going on. He answered.

"Yo, Dan."

"Is it true? Is Tyler dead?"

"Yeah." I could hear the pain in his voice.

"What happened?"

"We don't really know too much yet. All we know is that he's gone."

"What the fuck."

"I know. I'll keep you updated as soon as I hear anything."

"Thanks man. I got to get back to class."

"Later."

I slouched down in front of a row of lockers and put my head between my legs. I started crying. I never dealt with death like this before and I had no idea what to do. Death had finally taken someone very close to me.

Tyler was always the good kid. He played football and was very involved with school activities. He had a ton of friends and plenty of people who looked up to him. He wasn't like the rest of our friend group. The rest of us were drug addicts. He wasn't. Yet, for some reason he was the one that got taken. Why couldn't have been me? It should have been me. I should have been dead ten times over, but for some reason I was still here. Death didn't want me yet.

I had literally seen Tyler the night before. I had gone over to pick up Percocet from Mikey. I started getting high shortly after Anna and I had met up. It had nothing to do with Anna this time. I just wanted to get high, so I did. I had hung out with Tyler and Mikey last night. Now, he was gone. I would never see him again.

I went back to class. It was like everyone knew what had happened. The room was completely silent. I took a seat in my desk and just stared dead ahead of me. I felt a hand on my shoulder. It was one my friends, Hannah. She asked, "Are you okay?" I shook my head no. She knew what that meant. She knew that it was one of my close friends that died. She said, "I'm so sorry

Dan." It wasn't much, but at that time, it comforted me.

It came out that he had taken a deadly mixture of drugs that night. His brother had found him in the morning. I don't want to go into much more detail in order to respect him. All that mattered was that he was gone.

His funeral was later that week and it was one of the strangest experiences of my life. It was strange because it was heart wrenching. That wasn't the weird part though. The weird part was how many people were there that loved him. Everyone had come together in the wake of his death to support each other. It was amazing to see how many people had loved him. The combination of sadness and love was what was strange. I had never felt that before.

I had made it through his death and funeral without getting high. I did that for him. I didn't want to disrespect him by showing up to his funeral high as a kite. I just couldn't do that. Now that it was all over, I didn't know what was going to happen.

Drugs had finally taken one of my friends, but it didn't scare me. It only made me want to do more drugs. It was insane to think like that. I can't explain it, but that was how I felt. The day following the funeral, I went back to shooting heroin. It had been almost six months since I shot heroin, but I had found my way back to it.

Chapter 19

Death had finally found me. I had flirted with death for the last few years. We had danced together, but we never went further than that. Now, death had finally struck my life. Death had taken someone that had so much to live for and I was distraught.

At this point in my life, I had lost my grandmother and an unborn baby. I had come close to losing Anna and myself, but none of this compared to the loss of Tyler. Losing someone in their teenage years is difficult because they have so much life ahead of them. There is no reason that they should be taken so young, yet here we are. He was gone.

I dealt with his loss the same way that I dealt with everything else in my life, I got high. It was the only thing that made me feel better. There was no other way for me to get through this except by using. I was starting to use more and more. It wasn't just heroin, it was anything I could get my hands on.

My life was spiraling out of control and I had no way of catching it once again. Drugs had completely consumed me and my demons were winning the war. I wanted to drop out of school. I had no plans on going to college, so high school seemed pointless. I just wanted to drop out to continue selling drugs and getting high. I didn't really have any plans beyond that.

After Christmas, I decided to give school a little bit longer before I called it quits. My schedule had changed with the new semester and I now had a study hall for seventh period. There was a girl in my study hall that I had never talked to before. She was a small girl, probably about five-foot three. She had long brown hair that came down just above her waist. There was something about her that drew me in, just like Anna had.

This was the first girl that had really caught my attention since Anna. I had seen her before, we had been in some classes together. Her name was Hailey. For some reason, I had never noticed her before until now. Maybe it was because I had finally closed the door on Anna and was ready to move on.

I took a seat next to her on the first day of study hall. She looked over at me and gave me this little half smile. God, why do smiles always get me? It was almost the same smile that Anna used to give me, just a little different.

"Hey, I know we've never really met before, but my name's Dan."

"Yeah, I know who you are." She smiled, but never looked up from the book that she was reading.

"Oh, thanks for making me feel so important. Well, it's nice to meet you to Hailey."

She looked up from her book finally, "Oh, so you know who I am too?" She smiled.

"How could I not?"

"Well, you know who I am, but you never talked to me before. How come all of sudden you decided to?"

"I guess I just never had an opportunity. Then all of sudden, we're in the same study hall and there happens to be an open seat next to you. Now, here we are."

The teacher that was monitoring our study hall interrupted our conversation. "Anyone who wants to go to the art room to work on their projects may go now."

Hailey stood up and started to pack up her stuff. I stayed seated because I didn't take any art classes, so I had no reason to go. "You coming?" She asked.

"Um, no. I don't take art."

"So? Come on, the teacher loves me. She won't mind if you come with. We can continue our conversation there."

I was a little taken back. I hadn't expected for her to be interested from the start. Obviously, she was curious about me and wanted me to go with her. I wanted to get to know her and I grabbed my backpack and stood up. "Let's go."

We started walking towards the art room. At least I think we were. I had never taken an art class so I assumed Hailey was leading me to the right room.

She broke the silence, "I've heard a lot about you."

"Yeah, I get that a lot."

"I won't ask about any of it. I want to find out for myself though. You're kind of a mysterious person. Everyone talks about you, but you seem to keep to yourself for the most part."

"Yeah, trust me I wish people would mind their own business. The ones that talk about me don't know shit. I don't really hang out with many people from this school."

"I get it. I'm the same way. I'm sure you heard plenty of rumors about me freshmen year."

I was well aware of the rumors she was talking about. She had earned the reputation of sleeping around way back in our freshmen year. There was only one story I had heard, but it traveled through our school fast and it's hard to shake that off once it happens.

In fact, one of the times Anna and I had broken up. She had accused me of just using her for sex, which wasn't true. Anna had told me that if I had just wanted to fuck someone that I should have went after Hailey. It's funny how life comes full circle sometimes. Now, here I was talking to the girl that Anna had told me to go after.

"Yeah, we go to a small school and word travels fast. Let's make a deal."

"What's that?"

"We can talk about our rumors as much as we want, but we don't judge each other based on the truth involved in them."

She smiled, "You got a deal."

"So, what do you want to know?"

"Nothing yet. I just want to talk to you and spend the next period getting to know you."

"I think that sounds really good."

We spent the next period talking to each other about whatever came up. It felt really nice to have someone who was interested in me and my life. It had been so long since I really had a woman in my life that was actually healthy for me. I was very excited to have met her. The class ended with me getting her phone number.

We didn't stop talking since the time we met. I had texted her that night and our conversation just continued. I couldn't say that it was love at first sight because I had seen her before. Yet, I was still clouded by Anna. Now that I was free from her, I had really seen Hailey clearly for the first time and she was stunning. I had tripped and fallen for her immediately. I was enamored by her and I wanted her to be part of my life.

Part of the reason that I had fallen so quickly for her was that we shared the same demons. While we were texting that night, I had told her I was fucked up on Sub Oxone and she told me she was high on valium. It shouldn't have made me like her more, but it did. We shared something in common, drugs. I didn't go into too much depth with her about my drug usage because I didn't want her to know that I was a heroin junkie. In fact, I decided that I was going to stop doing heroin because of her. I didn't need it anymore if I had her in my life.

I had only known Hailey for about eight hours before I decided that I didn't want to do heroin anymore because of her. That may seem odd, but sometimes you meet someone and you just know that they were meant for you. That was how it felt with her.

I wasn't trying to replace Anna or make Anna mad by talking to Hailey. I was just trying to find happiness again. I believed that Hailey and I really had a chance. We clicked from the first words I said to her and it just went on from there.

The next day at study hall, we decided to go to the library instead. No one was ever in the library, so we would have it to ourselves except for the librarian. That became our daily routine and we both looked forward to it every day. We also spent as much time with each other between classes as we possibly could. I saw her about four times throughout the day at school. It was perfect.

We decided that we were going to hangout that weekend. We hadn't made any plans, but I had bought tickets to go see some horror movie. I didn't really care what it was, I just wanted to spend time with her. I had told her that I would pick her up from her house at seven. I was in the car now on my way to pick her up for our first date.

I was excited and nervous. The same butterflies that Anna used to give me were coming back as I got closer to her house. I knew that meant that she was special, just like Anna. I don't like comparing her to Anna because she was nothing like her, but it's the only comparison I had.

I pulled up to her house. I got out of the car and went to the front door and knocked. I could hear footsteps shuffling around in the house. Then Hailey opened the door.

"Why didn't you just text me that you were here?"

"I guess I'm old fashioned. I wanted to come get you."

"You're different."

"Why's that?"

"I don't mean it in a bad way. You're just different than any other guy I've talked to. Don't worry, I like it."

I grinned, "Thanks. So, are you ready to go?"

"Yeah, where are we going?"

"I figured we could go see a movie."

"We could or do you want to go out to dinner with some of my friends?"

"I would love to, but I actually already bought the tickets. We can do dinner the next time."

"Oh, so you think there's going to be a next time already?"She said jokingly.

"Well, I hope so at least. Come on let's go."

We walked to the car and got in. It was about a twenty-minute drive to the movie theater so we had some time to kill. I had come prepared to break the ice during the ride.

"I brought you something."

"What's that?"

I reached into my center console and pulled out a blunt that I had rolled earlier. She smiled when she saw it.

"You know me so well already."

I lit the blunt and handed it to her. I put music on for us to listen to as we smoked. The song that came on from my playlist was a song by Wiz Khalifa. Her face lit up when she heard it.

"Where the fuck did you come from? You're a gentleman, you smoke weed and you jam to Wiz. Where have you been all my life?"

"Apparently right in front of you, we just never crossed paths."

"So, let's go ahead and get this out of the way. We haven't talked about the rumors about either of us yet and I really want to know what happened with you and Anna?"

"Well, I'm sure anything you heard was her side of the story. I never ran my mouth about our relationship. I'm not like that. I keep my personal matters to myself. So, anything you heard wasn't from me."

"She made you out to look crazy and then you switched schools, which doesn't really add up to me. Then, you came back. There's got to be a good story to that."

"It depends how you define good. Long story short, she was shooting heroin freshmen year. She tried to kill herself. She overdosed three times while we were together. Last, but not least, she got an abortion without telling me. I'm happy to tell you more if..."

Hailey cut me off, "I think you're allowed to be a little crazy after all that.

I have her a glancing look.

"I... I didn't mean it like that. No one should ever have to deal with what you did, but life happens. I respect that you didn't put the real story out there for everyone and accepted the bullshit rumors for what they were. She put you through hell and you still never said a bad word about her."

"Thank you for that."

"So, do you want to know about the rumors about me?"

"Listen, that was three years ago now. I honestly don't care what happened in your past. I only care about what's happening now. We all have our baggage. I'll always accept yours if you always accept mine. I don't need to know unless you really want to tell me. Sometimes that past is better left in the past."

"Once again, where have you been all my life."

She rested her arm on the center console and I reached down and grabbed her hand. I locked my fingers between hers. There were no more words that needed to be said. We enjoyed the rest of the ride listening to music and passing the blunt back and forth.

We went into the movie and I immediately put my arm around her. She nuzzled up against me and we sat just like that for the entirety of the movie. It was perfect. It was technically our first date and it went just how I wanted it to.

I took her back home after the movie. On our way back, we talked about how shitty the movie was, but how nice it was to finally hang out outside of school. I had only known Hailey for a week, but it already felt like I had known her my entire life. On that ride home, I decided that I wanted her to be a part of my life. I thought it was too soon to throw that on her though. I decided to keep it to myself for a little while longer.

When we got back to her house she asked, "So, are you going to walk me back in as well?"

"Of course."

"Good, you didn't get to meet my parents when you picked me up, but my mom's home now, so you can meet her. She would have loved that you came to the door to get me."

"Damn, meeting the parents already? Things are moving fast."

"Shut up." She giggled.

We got out of the car and started walking inside. She opened the garage door so we could go inside. As soon as she stepped into the garage she turned around and looked up at me. I put my hands around her hips and pulled her closer to me as I leaned my head down towards hers. Our lips met and we had our first kiss.

She pulled her head back after a minute, "I've been wanting to do that since the day we met."

"Me too." I pulled her head back towards mine for one more kiss before we went in to see her mom. "Let's go meet your mom."

Hailey saved me, at least for a little while. I had stopped doing heroin for her. I also stopped selling drugs. The day after our first date, she asked me to stop selling. I didn't even have to think about it. I would do anything for her. She was also the reason that I decided to not drop out of school.

It's crazy how one person can change your life so quickly. Sometimes it's for the better and sometimes it's for the worse. Anna had changed my life for the worse so quickly. Yet, Hailey was the opposite. She had made my life immensely better in the span of a week.

Hailey never knew about my struggles with drugs. She knew I got high, but she never knew the extent of it. I never planned to tell her either. For now, I was done with heroin and would do pills here and there. I never wanted Hailey to know that side of me. She didn't need to. I planned to never be that person again. I was going to be a better person for Hailey.

Two weeks after our first date, Hailey and I started dating officially. That meant that now everyone at our school knew that we were an item. We spent every second we could together at school and people noticed quickly that we were together.

I was truly happy. I hadn't done heroin since we started talking. I didn't care about it anymore. I only cared about Hailey. My world no longer revolved around drugs, it only revolved around her. I had finally found something besides drugs that filled the void that Anna had left in me and it was Hailey. She made me feel whole again.

We spent as much time as we could together outside of school as well. We spent a lot of time at her house hanging out with her mom and her brother. Her brother was physically disabled and required a lot of care. So, sometimes we spent time at her house just to watch her brother.

Hailey had come into my life quickly and everything in my life was once again flipped upside down or should I say right side up. Everything felt normal for once. The chaos that had ruled my life for so long had finally dissipated. Now, it was just Hailey and me.

Chapter 20

My life had been centered around chaos since I turned fifteen. So, it had been three years that my life had been nothing but chaos. Chaos is unpredictable and confusing, but there is something beautiful about it, something I love. Chaos enables life to be complex. It allows life to be exciting and dreadful. The ups and downs of chaos is just like the highs and lows of using drugs. Chaos and drug use go hand-in-hand. I guess that's why I love chaos.

For now, my life was anything but chaotic. Everyday life for me was rather predictable. I would wake up, text Hailey, go to school, spend my study hall with Hailey, and then go home. After school, I would either go to work or go hang out with Hailey. Then, I would go to sleep and do it all again. Life was simple and I was enjoying it, but chaos always finds its way back to me or I seek it out. I'm not really sure which, but no matter what I do, chaos always finds its way back into my life.

Hailey and I had been dating for two months and everything was spectacular. There was nothing wrong in my life. I had finally moved on from Anna. She never even crossed my mind anymore. Also, I had dealt with Tyler's death and kept on living. Hailey had helped me turn my life completely around. She didn't even know that she saved me, but she did.

For some reason, I decided to go back to heroin. I can't even explain why. Just one night, it seemed like a good idea. I wanted to feel it running through my veins once again. I figured, what would be the harm in shooting heroin one more time?

So, that's what I did. I went and got a bundle of heroin and a bag of needles. I went through the ritual of preparing the shot of heroin. Then came my favorite part. I stretched out my left arm and decided which vein I was going to hit. I slid the needle in and pulled back on the plunger. I watched as blood filled the syringe. I slowly depressed the plunger, allowing the heroin to enter my blood system.

That was my favorite part of shooting heroin. Just staring at the blood in the syringe knowing that all I had to do was depress the plunger and allow myself to feel heaven. I had missed heroin and didn't even realize it. I had been so consumed with Hailey that heroin had faded from my mind. I didn't realize I missed it until it was in my veins again. This time, heroin really had me.

My relationship with Hailey continued without her knowing of my heroin use. On this heroin binge, I used for a month straight. I was getting high every day before school and immediately after school. My last shot of heroin was always around ten at night and then I would pass out.

I had started selling drugs again. Hailey did know about that. I had explained to her that I needed the money and it was as simple as that. I told her I wanted to save up for a new car and that selling drugs was the quickest way to save. She thought that I was just selling weed, but once again I was selling anything that people would buy. I needed to fund my heroin habit.

I'm not sure how Hailey didn't know that I was using heroin. She would ask about the track marks on my arm and I would tell her that I did something to it at work. She would accept that answer, maybe just because she didn't know any better. Also, she might not have wanted to believe that I was junkie. Her mom would also comment on how tired I always was. That was because I would be nodding off while spending time at her house.

It's not easy to hide being a heroin addict, but when people don't know the signs, it is easy to dismiss them as something simple. No one knew about my heroin use this time. I was keeping it to myself. I didn't want anyone to know that I had fallen back down the rabbit hole of heroin.

My month-long binge ended abruptly. I had run out of heroin one night and decided that I wasn't going to get any the next day. I woke up and went to school, but I got increasingly sick throughout the day. I went to the nurse's office and went home early.

By the time I got home, I was deathly ill. I couldn't eat or drink without vomiting. I couldn't even smoke a cigarette because that just induced vomiting as well. My whole body ached and there was nothing I could do to make it better. I tried getting some sleep, but I couldn't get comfortable and I barely got any sleep that night.

The next few days continued in the same manner. My sickness didn't get any worse, but it didn't get better either. My parents didn't know what to do because I hadn't taken in any food or liquid in almost three days. They decided that I needed to go to the hospital. They took me and the hospital immediately put me on a saline drip to rehydrate me. In total, I received six bags of saline. They told me that if I had waited any longer some of my organs would have started to fail.

After the hospital trip, I felt better immediately. I didn't realize it until I got home from the hospital, but something in my brain clicked. I had been withdrawing from heroin. I had never gone through withdrawals before so I didn't know what it was like. I didn't realize that my body needed heroin to function. My body was reacting to not having heroin and that's why I was so sick. That was the first time I ever withdrew.

After my realization, I told myself that I would never do heroin again. The withdrawal was excruciating and I never wanted to feel that again. I thought that after going through withdrawal that I would never want to do heroin again, but I was wrong. Heroin had its hold on me and it had no intention of letting go.

I only lasted about a week until I gave in to my craving for heroin. I was completely powerless over it. No matter what I did, heroin was in my head calling for me to come back. There was no way to escape the calls except to give in. It was the only way to quiet the voices.

Graduation had finally come. I was finally going to graduate and be done with school. I had no plans of going college. In fact, I had no plans at all. All I wanted to do was shoot heroin. I had told everybody that I planned to join the military after summer, but I didn't really want to do that. The only plan I had was to shoot heroin.

At our graduation, everyone walked to their seats with a classmate. It was a procession line more or less and somehow Hailey and I got paired together. We were going to walk into graduation at each other's side. It was one of those moments that made me think that maybe there really is a god. Here I was a junkie, who six months ago was going to drop out of school. Yet somehow, I ended up meeting Hailey and she saved me. She got me to turn my life around, even if it only lasted a few months. Now, Hailey and I were going to walk into graduation together. I was going to walk in with the girl that was the only reason I was still here.

It's moments like these that really make me think. I thought that maybe I should tell her everything. I wanted to tell her that I was a heroin addict and couldn't stop getting high. I needed her help. I needed her more than ever, but I couldn't do it. I knew it would cause her too much pain and I didn't want to do that to her. So, I decided to keep it a secret.

Graduation was a happy, but sad event. Hailey had plans to go to college, so I knew I really only had her for the rest of the summer. We never even discussed what would become of us when she went off to college. We just enjoyed the time together that we had. We would deal with her leaving when the time came. So, I enjoyed graduation just the same way. We walked in together and I had the biggest smile that I ever smiled on my face. It was one of the happiest moments of my life. I had actually made it through high school.

After graduation, my family and Hailey's family went out for lunch. It was the first time that our families had met each other. We talked about what both of our plans were for after the summer. She was going to college to study to be a nurse and I was going to the military. Well, at least that was what I told everyone because I couldn't tell them that I just planned to shoot heroin and sell drugs.

The month after graduation was a busy month for me. First, I had my high school's senior week. Then, I was going to Jamaica with my parents. When I came back from Jamaica I was leaving immediately to go to a senior week with some of Hailey's friends. The next three weeks were going to be filled with drinking and partying.

That was all I planned to do though. I wasn't going to do any hard drugs. We had already bought a bunch of liquor and weed for our senior week and that was all I planned to do. I wasn't going to ruin the fun by doing heroin.

Mark and I had gotten a hotel for the first senior week. We were going down a day later than everybody else because I had to work that Saturday. So, that Sunday we left for Ocean City, Maryland. When we got down, we checked into the hotel and brought all of our stuff inside. We placed the bottles of liquor we brought in the fridge and we put our weed in the nightstand. We were prepared to party that week.

Mark was planning to stay out a few of the nights so that Hailey could spend the night in the hotel with me. It was actually her birthday that week as well. So, her and I were going to go out to dinner to celebrate.

The week overall was more fun that I could have imagined. Although, I was withdrawing through most of it. I fought the withdrawal by drinking, which didn't really help. Yet, it made it a little bit more manageable. The withdrawal wasn't as bad as the last time though. I managed to get through that week without doing any hard drugs. All I did was smoke weed and drink.

The most significant thing that happened that week was one night Hailey and I were heading back to my hotel. We had both been drinking and we started talking about our relationship.

"I'm so thankful you came into my life." She said.

"Me too. I just wish we would have met sooner, but I guess everything happens for a reason."

"Yes, it does. So, how much do you like me?"

"I love you to the moon and back." Fuck, I didn't mean to say that. I meant it, but those were not the words that I meant to come out of my mouth. I had slipped. I didn't want to tell her I loved her by accident, but that was what had happened.

"Did you just say you love me?"

"Yeah, I meant to say I like you to the moon and back. I guess drunk words are sober thoughts though because that's the truth. I really do love you. I had been waiting for the right time to tell you and I guess that time is now."

She stared out the car window for a minute. She didn't reply, which was okay because I didn't want her to say anything that she didn't mean.

"I'm not quite ready to say it back."

"I don't want you to ever tell me something you don't mean. I'd always rather the hard truth than an easy lie."

"That's why you're the perfect person."

The rest of the car ride was spent in silence. We got back to the hotel and had a few more drinks before we crawled into bed. We laid there in each other's arms watching something on T.V. The night ended with us having sex and falling asleep next to each other.

The next night, she asked me to go outside with her at the party we were at. We walked out on to a balcony that overlooked the ocean. You could feel the breeze coming off the water and hear the waves breaking on the sand. The moon illuminated the sky and added the icing on the cake for a beautiful night.

"So, I've been thinking about what you told me last night."

I just stared at her. I wanted her to keep talking.

"I just needed a little time to think about everything. I honestly hadn't thought about it before you said it, so I didn't want to just blurt it out. What I'm trying to say is that I love you too."

I grabbed her around the waist and pulled her in close to me. I kissed her on the forehead and whispered in her ear, "I will always love you. No matter what happens, that will never change. Once I love someone, I love them for the rest of my life."

It was amazing to finally know that Hailey felt the same way that I did. We were in love. She told me she loved me on the last night of senior week. It was the perfect ending to the week.

The day we came back, the first thing I did was go get heroin. I hadn't got high in almost a week. Yet again, heroin was calling me. It didn't matter how many times I withdrew, I couldn't leave heroin alone. It felt like my relationship with Anna. It was completely toxic, but when I had it, everything was perfect in the world. All the chaos was worth the outcome. I had convinced myself that the means justified the ends.

I had a week before we left for Jamaica. That week consisted of me going to work, shooting heroin and hanging out with Hailey. That was what my life had become. Everything revolved around heroin though. Heroin was my top priority.

It was time to leave for Jamaica. I was going with my parents, but I was excited because you only have to be eighteen to drink there and I was now eighteen. That meant that I was going to be drunk the entire time there.

That week wasn't going to go as planned though. The third night that we were there, I got a call from Hailey. She was crying.

"What's wrong?"

"Ryan's dead."

Ryan was a friend of both of us. He was a junkie like me. We weren't that close, but I considered us friends. We bought and sold drugs from each other and had built a friendship on that. So, when she told me he was dead, I already knew what it was. Yet, I had to ask anyway.

"What happened?'

"He went into cardiac arrest and they couldn't save him. They're having a memorial for him at school tomorrow."

"Fuck, I'm sorry that I can't be there."

"It's okay. I'll be okay."

Eighteen-year-old kids don't just go into cardiac arrest. I knew that his death was drug related and it weighed heavy on me. He was now the second person that I had lost to drugs. Two kids were taken way too early from this life and brought to whatever waits for us after this life. Two families had been destroyed and would never truly recover from the loss of their sons.

I heard something a long time ago that said, "When someone dies, it just means that God needed them more than we do." I don't believe in God, but for some reason I find comfort in those words. Maybe that means I do believe in God, but who knows. For me, it just means that for some reason they had to go alone into that quiet night.

The last senior week that I was going on was with Hailey and some of her friends. It was going to be a quiet week. We planned to just drink and party at the house. I had come back from Jamaica on a Wednesday and was going down to senior week that night. Before I left, I went and picked up Sub Oxone for the week. I wasn't able to get heroin, so this was the next best thing. It would keep me from thinking about heroin, which would have to be enough.

At this point, I shot everything. It didn't matter what drug it was, I was putting it in a needle and into my vein. Therefore, I was going to be shooting Sub Oxone for the rest of that week and I would have to hide it from everyone there.

The rest of that week went as planned. Except I met someone that week that would spin my life even more out of control. One of Hailey's friends who was there happened to be a drug dealer. His name was Tanner and he only sold weed, but he sold a lot of weed. We hung out together a lot that week and became friends. He asked me if I wanted to sell for him when we got back and without hesitation I agreed.

That was the end of any good times I would have. The next two months of my life would be the darkest times that I ever went through. Meeting Tanner would be one of the worst things that ever happened to me. The end was near for me and I didn't know what lay ahead.

Chapter 21

I was nearing the end of the road, but I didn't know that yet. The road was just continuing to grow darker and more secluded. I was happily traveling down the road though. I didn't know any better. I mean, I did, but I didn't know if there was any other way to go.

Life happens. Decisions are made. Consequences follow. That's how life goes. We have no control over what happens in our life, but we do have control over the decisions we make based on our circumstances. Sometimes the consequences are clear and defined, but sometimes we have to take a leap of faith and hope that we make the right decision. That's the beauty of life and death. The unknown.

I had been traveling down this unknown road for some time now. Eventually, I would find myself at a fork in the road. Two options, many different outcomes. What would I decide?

After my last senior week, I went home and went back to work. I was back to the chaos of my life. I had been able to escape it for a little while, but as always, the chaos continues. Shortly after coming home, I reached out to Tanner to meet up with him. He told me to come over that night to talk.

I pulled up to his house. He lived in a townhome with his mom. I guess his mom knew what he did or she just didn't care. Either way it was none of my business. My business was to sell weed for him.

He came to the door to get me and lead me up to his bedroom. There was a couch in his room and I took a seat next to him on the couch. We exchanged the typical bullshit conversation before we got down to business. He even offered me a hit off his bong, I was already high as a kite. I had shot up in the car before coming in, but I couldn't refuse free weed.

"So, you've sold before?"

"Yeah, nothing crazy. I've been selling for a while now."

"Check this shit out."

He went into his closet and pulled out one of those large storage containers. He slid it across the floor to me. "Open it up."

I did as he said. As I lifted the lid on the container, the smell of weed enveloped the room. The whole container was full of weed.

"I get my shipments from Cali. I typically get fifty pounds at a time. How much do you think you can move?"

I didn't reply at first. My only thought was that I barely know this kid and he just showed me a large amount of weed. I thought he was an idiot for that. I could have robbed him right then and there if I was prepared for that, but I wasn't. I was a little worried about selling for him because being this upfront with me seemed stupid. Yet, I needed the money and I couldn't refuse.

"I can move about a pound week. If you can consistently supply me, maybe quicker."

"I never run out. My next shipment comes when I'm down to five pounds."

"So, how much for a pound?"

"Twenty-two hundred."

"I don't have that on me."

"It's cool. I'll front it to you and I'll see you in a week. If you flip it quicker, let me know and I'll give you the next one."

"Sounds like a deal to me."

He proceeded to weigh out a pound of weed for me. Once he was done, I shook his hand and headed out to my car. In my trunk, I kept a duffle bag full of coffee beans. It helped to conceal the smell of weed. I opened my trunk and placed the weed into the bag.

I would be making one thousand dollars for every pound I sold. I had a few people that would take four ounces at a time. Therefore, I was now making an extra thousand every week and that just meant more heroin. I thought it was the best thing to happen to me.

Hailey was upset that I started working for Tanner, but she let it go eventually. She knew that I was going to do whether she agreed with it or not. She was just happy that I didn't hide it from her. She still had no idea that the reason I needed to sell drugs was to fund my heroin habit. She would find out soon enough though.

Once I started working for Tanner, I had enough money to do a bundle of heroin every day. My life quickly got unmanageable and I quit my job lifeguarding. There was no point in me going to my job when I could make way more if I was just selling drugs.

I didn't tell my parents that I quit my job. I would just leave the house like I was going to work and go hang out with my friends all day and get high. I would sell the weed, get my heroin and spend the days nodding out. It was good while it lasted, but it didn't last very long.

One night I came home and the door to my house was locked. I tried the garage door code and it didn't open. I was confused. My phone was dead, so I couldn't call my parents to let me in. I walked over to the neighbor's house and asked to use their phone.

"Hey mom, I think I got locked out."

"Dan, we found drugs in the basement. You're no longer welcome at our house."

"Are you serious?"

"Yes, goodbye."

My mom spoke through tears. She must have found the heroin and needles that I left in the basement. Now, my parents knew about my drug use. It must have killed them. They knew I wasn't sober anymore. They had caught me drinking about a year ago, but they had no idea I was back on heroin. It must have broken their hearts finding my stash.

I left the neighbor's house and called Mark. He said I could spend the night. So, at least I would have some where to sleep that night. I had no idea what I was going to do. My heroin addiction was getting heavier and I no longer had a place to live.

That night, I came to the conclusion that I was near the end of my run. I was going to have to go to rehab soon. My world was crashing and burring around me. It seemed like the only solution. That meant that Hailey was going to find out what was going on. I wasn't ready to tell her yet, but I knew I had to. There was no way around it anymore.

I also decided that I wasn't going to pay Tanner back for the last pound that he had fronted me. I was going to keep the money and use it for the next couple days. I planned to get a hotel room and shoot heroin until I was out of money. I had about half a pound left and a thousand dollars to my name. I knew that I could easily sell the other half pound the next day for another twelve hundred. That meant that I could get high for about another week before I had to face rehab.

The next few days I bounced between people's couches and hotels. I called my parents and told them that I needed to go to rehab. They told me that I could come home if I was willing to go to treatment. I was, but I told them I would be home the next day. I wanted to get high for one more night.

After I got off the phone with my parents, I went and got three bundles of heroin. That was going to be the last time that I picked up heroin. This was my final hoorah. After I picked up, I went and checked into a hotel room.

I was not in a good state of mind. I knew that I could no longer get high and I didn't know if I could go on with life without getting high. I was debating on whether or not I should shoot enough heroin to kill myself.

I decided that I wasn't going to intentionally kill myself, but if I died, I was okay with that. That day, I shot more heroin than I ever had. The night ended with me loading six bags of heroin into a needle. I had never done more than a two-bag shot before. The reason I only shot two at a time was because I was too scared to overdose. Now, that the fear was gone. I didn't care if I woke up the next day.

That was the last shot of heroin that I took. I honestly did not think that I would make it through the night, but I did. I woke up the next morning and I had to get on with my life. My parents and I said we would meet for breakfast to talk before I came home.

We met for breakfast at a local diner. By the time I got there, my parents were already there. I walked inside and found the table that they were seated at. They were happy to see me alive and well. They wanted to discuss what my plan was. My plan was to go back to work and keep my mind occupied with work. They didn't think that would work, but were willing to try. We agreed that if things didn't work out, I was going to have to go to rehab.

The next few days I spent at my parents withdrawing yet again. I had already lined up two new jobs for myself. One was a job that I quit about six months ago. They were willing to let me come back. The other was a new lifeguarding job. I was set to start work at the beginning of the next week.

I didn't even make it until my jobs started before I got high again. The withdrawals were too much for me. I gave in and went over to one of my dealer's houses. I told my parents that I was going to a meeting so that I could leave the house.

I went over to his house and he had a bundle of heroin waiting for me. I shot up at his house and I immediately was no longer sick. That's the beauty of heroin withdrawal. You know what the cause is and the medicine is easily accessible. One shot of the medicine makes everything better. I was okay again.

I continued to use heroin without my parents catching on. I began my new jobs, but that only lasted a few days. On my fourth day of work lifeguarding, I went to leave and realized that my car wasn't there. I grabbed my phone to call my mom.

"Hey, where's my car?"

"We suspected that you were using again. We came to get your car so we could search it. We found heroin. You're going to have to go to rehab."

I sighed. "I know. Can you come pick me up?"

"Are you willing to go to rehab?"

"Yes, I need to."

"Your dad will be there in a little bit to pick you up. We love you."

"Thanks, I love you too."

That was it. This was the end of the road. The years of using drugs had lead up to this moment. Now, I was just going to have to wait to get into a rehab. I was also going to have to explain everything to Hailey. She was supposed to come over that night anyway, so I figured I would tell her everything then. This wasn't going to be pretty.

By the time I got home, my mom had already been calling rehabs to try to find one for me to go to. She had found one that had an open bed and I could go the next day. She asked if that was okay with me and I told her that was fine.

Hailey arrived about an hour later and we went down into the basement. We sat down on the couch and I got ready to spill the secret that I had been hiding from her for so long. I took one last deep breath before I told her everything.

"So, there's something that I need to tell you. I want to apologize before I start for not telling you this sooner." I could tell she was already fighting back tears. I think she already had an idea of what I was about to say.

"I've been shooting heroin for the past six months. When we first started talking, I had stopped doing heroin because of you. Then one day, I just decided that I needed heroin again. I don't know why, but I went back to it. I haven't been able to stop since. I'm going to rehab tomorrow to try to get my life back together."

She started crying. She spoke through her tears, "I know you've had your struggles. I wish you would have told me so that we could have gotten through this together."

I put my arm around her and tried to comfort her. "I know. I fucked up. I always fuck up."

"I thought you and I were going to be together forever, but you chose heroin over me."

She was right. I had done to her exactly what Anna had done to me. I hated myself for it, but heroin gave me something that she never could. I now realized what it was like to be on the other side of this conversation.

"I know it doesn't change anything, but I really am sorry."

"I can't go through this with you. I'm leaving for college soon and I don't think we should be together anymore. We can still be friends, but I can't be your girlfriend anymore. This is all too much for me to handle. I really do want to help you through this though."

I started fighting back tears. I could see how much pain I had caused the girl I loved and it cut right through me. I wish that heroin had never come into my life, but maybe I never would have met her had it not. So, this was where we stood.

"Thank you for that."

We didn't speak after that. She just stayed nuzzled against me. We were holding each other for the last time. We both knew that once we let go of our embrace, we would never feel each other again. I'm not sure how long we stayed like that for, but I know it wasn't long enough. I didn't want to ever let go of her, but she knew she had to let go of me.

Eventually she said, "I have to go."

I walked her out to the car and gave her one last hug. While I had her in my arms, I whispered in her ear, "I will always love you no matter what happens. I will always be here for you."

"I love you too."

I kissed her on the forehead. She got into her car and I watched as she drove away. I didn't know what her future held for her, but I knew it didn't include me. I was watching her drive right out of my life. That was the end of our story, almost.

The next day came and I was packing my bags to go to rehab. I was going through withdrawal already and I didn't want to go to rehab withdrawing. I had a feeling that my parents still had the heroin they found when they kicked me out. I decided that I was going to try to get it from my mom. I went to go talk to her.

"Mom, I have something I need to ask you."

"What's that?"

"Do you still have the heroin that you found in the basement."

"Um, yes. Why?"

"I'm going through withdrawal and I need to get high one more time before I go. Could I please have it?"

"Absolutely not. There's no way I'm condoning you shooting heroin."

"Well, I'm not going until I get high. So, either you're going to let me go buy heroin or you can give me what you have."

"Let me call the rehab and see what they say."

I sat down on the couch and listened as my mom called the rehab. I knew it killed her that I had asked for the heroin, but I really needed it. She hadn't called my bluff either. I was completely out of money. There was no way for me to buy heroin. The only way I was going to get high again was if she gave me what she had.

She came back a few minutes later. "They said, if you promise to go after that it's okay for me to give it to you."

"I really do want to go to rehab. I just need one more high."

"Are you ready to leave after you use it?"

"Yeah, my bags are packed. I'm all ready to go."

"Okay, I'll go get it."

She went out to the garage. I'm not sure where she had been keeping the heroin, but it was either hidden in the garage or in her car. She came back with two bags of heroin in her hand. She placed it on the coffee table in front of me. Tears were streaming down her face.

"There you go. Do what you need to do. I'll be waiting in the car for you."

"Thank you."

I picked up the bags of heroin and went down into the basement. I retrieved a needle from my hiding spot and prepared my last shot of heroin. I went through the ritual of preparing to shoot up one last time. Then, I felt the heroin enter my veins, one last time.

I went back upstairs and grabbed my suitcase. I headed out to the car and threw my bag into the truck and hopped in the front seat with my mom.

"You're not going to overdose are you?"

"No, mom. That wasn't very much heroin. I'll be okay."

"I just needed to ask."

We began the drive to the rehab. It was about forty-five minutes away. The rehab was in a shitty part of town, but it was the only place that had an open bed. I really didn't care where I went to get help. I just needed help. Rehab was the only option left for me. If it didn't work this time, I don't know what I would do. I couldn't live with shooting heroin, but I couldn't live without either. I was at yet another crossroad.

So much had happened throughout the last four years. Me going to rehab was the culmination of all those events. I had fallen in love with a heroin addict, watched her try to kill herself, dealt with her claiming she was overdosing multiple times, she killed my child, I tried numerous drugs, I went to rehab, I relapsed and shot heroin, I lost a bestfriend, I fell in love with the perfect girl, I went back to heroin, I lost the perfect girl and now I was on my way to rehab.

I still believe that everything happens for a reason and that I had to experience all of that. I don't know why I needed to, but everything is life is a lesson. The chaos that I went through was one of the most valuable lessons that I ever learned. I gained wisdom that people search their whole lives for. I had learned so much in four short years. Those experiences molded me into the person I am today.

Chapter 22

This was going to be my second stay at a rehab. I expected everything to be similar to my first experience. The only difference this time was that I was at an adult rehab. I knew what to expect and I was okay with it. I was at a point where I knew I needed help. The only way for me to get sober was by going to rehab. I had tried to kick heroin a few times, but it never lasted. Rehab was my last hope.

I got checked into the rehab and my mom left to go home. I assumed tonight would be her first good night's sleep in a long time. The last few weeks while I was home, my parents would check on me throughout the night to make sure that I was still breathing. Now, I was in a safe environment, which would give them some peace of mind.

I was put on Sub Oxone to help with the detox and withdrawals. They put me on a few other medications as well. I don't remember exactly what they were, but they were supposed to help with the withdrawals as well.

Sub Oxone is supposed to be used as a maintenance drug to get off of heroin. It can also be used to get high as well. I had only used it in the past to get high. Now, I was taking it to ween myself off of heroin. They started me on a rather high dose of twenty-four milligrams a day, which would eventually taper down to nothing after five days.

The first day, the dose of Sub Oxone was enough to get me feeling good. I wasn't high, but I didn't have any of my normal withdrawal symptoms. I was in the detox unit, which meant I could come and go from meetings or therapy as I pleased. I could go rest whenever I felt the need. I would be in there for the first three days until I was through the worst of the withdrawal symptoms. After that, I would be put into my group and would have to follow all the rules.

This rehab was pretty much the same as my first one. The only real difference was that the males and females were not separated. We were allowed to talk to each other and were around each other all day.

I was one of the youngest people there. There were a few people close to my age, but I was the youngest. I kept to myself for the most part. I really had no interest in talking to people there. I was there to get better, not to make friends. You don't really make any friends in places like this anyway. You might make some acquaintances, but when you leave you leave them there.

I had made it through the detox period and was moved into a group. That meant that I was now allowed to use the phone at night to make phone calls. I was excited because that meant that I was finally going to be able to talk to Hailey. This had been the longest i went without talking to her since we had met.

That night, I called her. She answered immediately.

"Hey, It's Dan."

"Oh. Hey! How's everything going?"

"It's going. I don't really want to be here, but I know I have to be."

"Well, I'm glad you're there."

"It's so nice to hear your voice."

"Honestly, you too. I miss you."

"I miss you too. I wish that things had gone differently. I wish I didn't fuck up."

"Yeah, me too."

"So, I know this question is really random, but I've been thinking about it a lot lately."

"What's that?"

"I told you how many people I slept with, but I told you not to tell me. I want to know now."

"Why does it matter now?"

"I just want to know."

"I'm not going to tell you that now, Dan."

"Why not?"

"I don't think it matters."

"You probably don't want to tell me because the number is a lot. I know the stories about you. You're a whore."

I could hear her start to cry. "Why are you acting like this?"

"I wouldn't be if you just would have told me."

"I don't think we should talk anymore."

"Whatever."

"Goodbye, Dan."

I don't know what had come over me. I had been wanting to ask her that for a little while now. I'm not sure why, but I just wanted to know. I don't know why I snapped like that. I don't know why I treated her like that. After all, I loved her. Why would I ever say that to her?

That was the last conversation I ever had with Hailey. That was how our story ended, with me calling her a whore and her crying. I'm not proud of it at all and I wish things would have played out differently. For some reason, I had to ask that one question that really was none of my business anymore.

I still think about Hailey often. I wonder how she's doing and I hope she's happy. I hope that she learned a lesson from me. Most times when I think about her, I wonder what would have happened if I never went back to heroin. Would her and I still be together? I believed she was the one for me, but heroin had come between us. If heroin was eliminated from the equation, I believe we would still be together. I believe my life would look a lot different.

That's just a fantasy that I allow myself to play out sometimes. In reality, she's just another ghost. She doesn't haunt me the way that Anna does though. My memories with Hailey are happy memories. I try to remember how we were when we were together, not how we ended.

The next few days were tough for me. Hailey was now completely out of my life. I had no one. There was no one I could call that would want to talk to me. I was truly alone in the world, besides my parents of course. That's not the same though.

My thoughts had become darker and I didn't know if I wanted to live any longer. I began to fantasize about running away from rehab and overdosing on heroin. I played it all out in my head.

The rehab wasn't far from Philadelphia. My thoughts were that I could walk there and find a corner to panhandle on. Once I had enough money, I would go and buy a bundle of heroin. Once I had the heroin, I would shoot the whole bundle in one shot. It would definitely be enough to kill me.

I don't think I ever actually planned on doing it, but I really fucking wanted to. I just wanted to escape. I knew there was no way for me to continue being a heroin addict. Therefore, the only way for me to truly escape was to end it all. I really wanted to die, but for some reason I pushed through.

One day, there was a new girl at the rehab. I thought I recognized her, but couldn't quite place how I knew her. Then, it clicked. She was one of Mark's sister's friends. Her name was Marisa and she came over to talk to me on a smoke break.

We talked for a little bit about how we both ended up there. Neither of us knew that the other was heavily into drugs. The conversation ended with both of us wishing the best for each other. It's such a small world and it was really strange to see someone that I knew at rehab yet again.

I had gotten close with a few people there. The one's name was Kyle, he was about a year older than me. I should have never gotten close with him though because we soon started talking about leaving rehab to get high.

Talking about it soon turned into devising a plan on how to do it. We decided that we could leave the rehab, go get heroin and then come back. The rehab was in a shitty part of town. We knew that we could buy heroin somewhere near buy. We would get heroin, shoot it and then come back with no one being the wiser.

We decided that we were going to go that night. He had snuck some money in with him and we were going to use that to pay for it. He was okay with buying me some as long as I kept him company. The plan was to hop the fence at the night time smoke break. When we came back, we would enter through one of the side doors.

Night came and we made our move. We walked over to the darkest part of the area where we had our smoke breaks. We looked around to see if anyone was watching. We came to the conclusion that no one was looking and we made our move. We hopped the fence and took off running. I was following him and didn't stop running until he did. By the time we stopped, we were a few blocks from the rehab.

The first part of our plan had worked. Now, all we had to do was cop heroin. In shitty parts of town, you can just ask people who has dope. Dope is another word for heroin. It was summer time, so there was still a lot of people sitting out on their porches. We would walk past a house and just say, "Dope?"

For the most part, we got people who either didn't know or didn't want anything to do with two kids. We kept up our search and eventually got a positive response. I had asked, "Dope?" The response was, "You're not cops, are you?"

"Fuck, no. Do we look like cops?"

The guy came down off the porch to talk to us. "How much do you guys want?"

"We've got forty bucks on us."

"I'm not holding, but my homie is. He's in the hospital. I'll take you there and we can pick up from him."

"Perfect. How far is the hospital?"

"Five-minute walk."

He lead the way as both of us followed. When we got there, he told us to give him the money and he would go get it. We were hesitant because we didn't want him to take the money and run. We didn't have any other options though, so we handed him over the money and he went inside.

Five-minutes later he came back out and shook my hand. During the handshake, he transferred the heroin to me. I felt the bags in my hand and immediately put them in my pocket.

"Thanks man."

I looked at the time, it was eight fifty-five. We had to get to a pharmacy by nine. We had five minutes to get there and buy needles. We looked around to see if we could spot a CVS sign. There was nothing in sight. Someone walked out of the hospital. I asked them if there were any drug stores around. He said there was one three blocks that way and pointed in the general direction.

Kyle took off running and I followed him. We got there with a minute to spare. Kyle went in and got the needles. He came back out with a smile on his face. I knew that meant that we were both about to get high.

There was a park nearby and we walked over to one of the benches. That was where we were going to shoot the heroin. We both had two bags. Kyle had found a water bottle and that's what we were going to use to mix the powder with. We both prepared our shots and loaded them into the needle. I found the vein that I always loved to hit in the crook of my arm. I slipped the needle into it and pulled the plunger back. I saw blood flow into it and knew I hit a vein. I knew that I was about to feel heroin in me once again. I thought that I would never feel heroin again. Yet, here I was with a needle sticking out of my arm once again.

We began walking back to the rehab. We walked slowly. We were in no rush to get back. We had accomplished what we set out to do. We had both gotten high. We eventually made it back and walked towards the door we planned to enter through.

We pushed the door open and went upstairs to where we were supposed to be. A staff member stopped us on our way, "Where were you two?"

Fuck, we were caught. "We were in group."

"No, you weren't. You guys were missing. Come with me."

It turns out, they knew we had left. They split us up and put us in separate rooms. They sent a staff member in to talk to me. He took a seat at the desk and said, "So, where were you?"

I thought about lying, but we were caught. There was no way out of this one. "We left."

"Where did you go?"

"We went to get high."

"Are you high right now?"

"Yeah, we copped heroin."

"Thank you for your honesty. I'm going to have to wait until the director comes in tomorrow to figure out what to do with you."

"What's going to happen?"

"Most likely, you will be kicked out."

"Is there anything I can do to convince you to let me stay?"

"I'd recommend writing a letter to the director on why you think you should stay."

"Okay, thank you."

"You can go back to your group area now."

I walked up the stairs to the room where everyone hung out at night. It was a room with couches and a T.V. At night, we were allowed to watch movies and shows until we wanted to go to bed. It was already eleven and everyone was in bed.

There was an office next to the common room, where the night staff spent their shift. I walked into the office and asked for a pen and paper. She gave it to me and followed me into the common room.

I guess she had heard what happened because she started asking me why I did it. She wasn't questioning me, she was trying to help me. She wanted to help me through it. We talked for a little while as I started writing the letter. Eventually, I told her that I need to write this letter to improve my odds of not being kicked out. She obliged and transferred her focus to whatever show was on.

The letter I wrote poured my heart on to paper. It explained that I was a drug addict with nowhere to go. My parents didn't want me home and I had no one else. If I was kicked out I didn't know what would happen, but I knew it was nothing good. I begged and pleaded in that letter. It ended up being seven pieces of paper front and back. I'm sure I rambled on a little bit since I was still high. By the time I was done writing, I was content with what I wrote. I thought that if this didn't change their mind, nothing would.

I gave the letter to the staff member. She said that she would make sure that it got to the director first thing in the morning. After that, I went to sleep.

The next day, I was called into the director's office. We talked for a little while and the conversation ended with him allowing me to stay. He believed that I had made a poor choice, but that it shouldn't hinder my chances at staying sober. If I acted up at all, I would be kicked out though.

I was ecstatic that I was able to stay. I knew it was the only option for me. There was nothing left for me out in the real world. I needed rehab to teach me how to stay sober. The director had given me another chance and I wasn't going to waste it.

I had two weeks left of rehab and I was going to take it seriously. I was going to be completely open in therapy and groups. I knew I needed to do everything in my power to help myself stay sober. I thought that being open and honest was the best chance I had.

Over the next two weeks, I learned a lot about myself and how to stay sober. My parents and I decided that after rehab I was going to go to a recovery house. These were houses filled with recovering addicts that help you to start over. You go to the house and have to follow strict rules that are designed to acclimate you back into society.

I really wanted to go home, but my parents weren't letting me. The only option I had was a recovery house. I wasn't happy about it, but it was the only choice. My parents believed that it would give me the best chance of staying sober.

The morning that I was released from rehab, there was a van waiting to take me to the recovery house. The house was in a town called Levittown. I had never heard of it before and had no idea where I was going.

When we arrived, it looked like your typical home that a family would inhabit. The driver told me that we were here and he would walk me in. When we knocked on the door, a guy in his thirties answered.

"Hey, you must be the new guy."

"Yeah, I guess so."

"My names Jack. I'm the assistant house manager. That means I help make sure that everything here runs smoothly. Let's go sit down and go over some paperwork. I'll need you to sign a few things and I'll give you the run down on how this works."

We walked inside and sat down at the kitchen table. "So, have you ever been to a recovery house before?"

"No."

"I'll explain how all this works. When we're done talking, you need to read and sign those papers to say that you agree to all of it."

"Okay."

"The first thirty days that you are here, you are on blackout. This means that you can only leave the house for work and meetings. If you don't have a job, you have to leave the house from nine to four to look for a job. Once those thirty days are up, you are allowed to come and go as you please, but you do have a curfew of midnight. You haven't to sign the sign out book whenever you leave and write down where you are going. This is so we know where you are at all times. You will also be assigned a chore that you have to complete on a daily basis. Other than that, just get along with everyone in the house and don't get high. You will be drug tested randomly. Any questions?"

I had a few questions, but none I was going to ask him. My biggest question was how the fuck did I end up here. "No, I think I got it."

"Awesome, go ahead and sign those papers. Your room is just behind us. Go ahead and make yourself comfortable."

I was so uncomfortable. I had never lived anywhere besides my parents. Now, I was thrown into this house with a bunch of strangers. I had no idea how I was going to make it through this, but I had to try. I already wanted to leave and go get high.

As the day progressed, everyone else that lived there started to come back to the house. It turns out that a total of twelve people lived in the house. The age varied from eighteen to sixty and everyone came from different backgrounds. I had to share my room with three other people. I had the top bunk on the bunk beds. This was the most uncomfortable situation I had ever been in.

I got along with everyone in the house because we all shared basically the same stories. Granted, all of our stories were unique, but the common denominator was drugs. We had all gotten here because of some form of substance. How the stories played out varied, but they all ended the same.

Over the next few weeks, I followed all the rules. I did my chore, went on job search and went to a meeting every night. I thought I was doing well, but soon my obsession to use heroin came back. I couldn't stop thinking about shooting heroin. It slowly became all I thought about.

One day on job search, I was talking to someone else that lived in another recovery house. We decided that the next day we were going to go get high. We had made up our minds. The plan we set was to meet at the train station at nine thirty so we could catch the train into the city to get heroin.

That night, two guys showed up at the house. I was in my room alone and they came in. "Hello, are you Dan?"

"Yeah, that's me. What's up?"

"Anthony told us everything. He told us that the two of you planned to go get high tomorrow."

"Um, I haven't gotten high so I don't see what the problem is."

"You planned to go with someone from another house to go use, that's enough for us to kick you out of the house."

"Yeah, but I didn't get high. You can piss test me, I'm clean."

"You're missing the point, you planned to go get high tomorrow."

"Well, what do I need to do to not get kicked out?"

"You're going to have to tell us that you're not going to get high tomorrow or any day in the future."

"That's ridiculous. I'm a drug addict, not a fortune teller. I can't tell you what is going to happen tomorrow."

They looked at each other for a minute. "Just tell us that you won't follow through on your plan to use tomorrow and we will give you another chance."

"Fine, I won't get high tomorrow."

They could tell I was being a wise ass. I think they wanted to give me another chance because of how young I was. They didn't want to put me out on the streets. Yet, they should have because I didn't change my mind about going to get high the next day. I was still going to. I didn't care if someone came with me or not. My mind was made up.

The next day came and I walked to the train station to catch the train at ten. I got on the train that took me into Center City. From there, I had to catch another train to get to Kensington. Kensington is the heroin capital of the east coast. They call it an open air black market. You can get anything and everything you want there.

As soon as I got off the second train, I had people asking me if I wanted Sub Oxone and Xanax. I asked him where the closest dope block was and he pointed me in the right direction. Within five minutes of getting to Kensington, I had gotten my needles and heroin.

I went back to the train station and got the next train back to Center City. I didn't want to get high yet. I wanted to talk to my parents first. I wanted to try to convince them to let me come home. I wouldn't get high if they let me back home.

Once I got on the train that would take me back to Levittown, I called my dad.

"Hey."

"What's up Dan?"

"Can I please come home? I hate it here. All I want to do is get high."

"I don't think that's the right decision."

"I went and got heroin. I haven't used yet and I won't if you let me come home."

"Dan, please don't do that. We can't have you back here. Using won't change anything, it's only going to hurt you."

"Please, just let me come home."

"I'm sorry Dan, I have to go. I love you."

I hung up the phone. I decided that as soon as I got off the train, I was going to get high. Once we got to my stop, I got off the train. There was a little tunnel that went under the road once you were off the train. It was the perfect spot for me to shoot up. No one had gotten off at the stop with me, I was all alone.

I walked down the steps into the tunnel and sat on the last step. I grabbed everything out of my backpack that I needed. I had a water bottle, heroin and a needle on the step next to me. I took the water bottle cap off the bottle and place it between my legs. I ripped the top off of two bags of heroin and poured them into the cap. I filled the needle with twenty CC's of water and squirted it into the cap. I began to stir the heroin until it was completely dissolved in the water. I no longer used a cotton to filter the heroin because I didn't want to lose any heroin in the process. I drew the solution up into the needle and found a vein in my arm. I slipped the needle into my vein. I pulled back on the plunger and watched the blood fill the needle once again. I didn't hesitate before I pushed the plunger back down and felt the heroin enter my veins.

That would be the last time that I ever shot heroin. I didn't know it at the time, but that would be my last farewell. The last farewell almost killed me though. That wasn't why I finally stopped shooting heroin though. I no longer feared death, I welcomed it. If I had died that day, I would have been okay with it.

Chapter 23

I came to laying in grass. I had no idea where I was. The last thing I remembered was shooting two bags of heroin. I sat up and realized I had no shoes on. They were laying just in front of me. I was laying in the grass just on the other side of the train station. It was just next to a shopping center on a busy road. I must have fallen out.

Falling out is when you pass out from doing too much heroin. It is technically an overdose. You are able to come back around on your own though. It is as close to death as you can get without actually having to be revived by medical personnel.

I put my shoes back on and checked my phone. I had been out for almost an hour. I had no idea how know one called the police about someone passed out in the grass next to the road. I figured I needed to leave in case the police were on their way. I started walking back towards my recovery house.

I checked my phone and I had three missed calls from the manager of my recovery house. I called him back.

"Dan, where are you?"

"I'm on my way back to the house."

"Did you get high?"

I didn't respond right away. I thought about lying, but I knew he would give me a urine test when I returned. I figured I would save both of us the trouble. "I did."

"You're going to have to leave."

"I know. I'm coming back to grab my things."

I returned to the house and began packing a small bag to take with me. I wasn't taking all my stuff because I didn't want to carry all of it. Plus, I really didn't care about bringing it with me. It was just a bunch of clothes anyways. So, I threw a change of clothes in my backpack and left the house without saying a word to anyone.

I had nowhere to go. I had no plan. I was lost. Heroin had finally taken everything from me. I was actually homeless now. I went to a nearby shopping center and took a seat on the bench out front. I must have nodded off again because I woke up to someone shaking me.

"Yo dude, someone called the cops. You better get out of here."

It was some stranger. Someone must have called the cops since I passed out on the bench. I didn't have any more heroin on me, but I still had needles. I found the closest trash can and disposed of the needles.

I still had nowhere to go. So, I decided to call my dad to try to find a solution.

"Dad, I got kicked out of the house. I don't know what to do."

"You made your bed, now you're going to have to sleep in it."

"Please let me come home."

"No, there's nothing I can do for you."

I hung up the phone. I needed to come up with a plan. I couldn't be homeless. I wasn't built for it. I had no desire to keep getting high and living on the streets. I had to figure something out quickly. The problem was that I had no one to get me out of this situation. I was going to have to figure it out on my own.

I began wandering around town for a little while. I walked to Wawa and stole a few small items so that I had something to eat. By now, it was about ten at night. I was tired and needed to find somewhere to sleep. I stumbled upon a bus stop and decided that was the best place for me to get some rest.

Before I fell asleep, I decided that the next day I would go to the local hospital. They would be able to help me get into another rehab. It was the only solution that I had. I had nowhere else to go and they were the only people that could help me.

I slept at the bus stop that night and woke up early in the morning. I had no idea what time it was because my phone had died. I knew it was around six in the morning because the sun was starting to come up. I grabbed my bag and started walking towards the hospital.

The hospital was not too far away. It was only about a thirty-minute walk. When I got there, I went to the emergency room to check myself in. I told them that I was drug addict and needed to get into a rehab.

They checked me in and took me into a room. I fell asleep almost immediately. Throughout the day, people came in to talk to me about my drug use and what I wanted to do. I told them everything about my using habits and that I needed to get into a rehab.

At some point during the day, they came in and told me they had gotten me a bed at a rehab and that I would go the next day. They would take me there by ambulance. After I heard that, I was comforted because I had a solution to my problem. I slept the rest of the time I was there.

They woke me up the next day and told me that it was time to go. I didn't even ask where I was going. I didn't care. All I cared about was that I was getting into a rehab. They loaded me into the ambulance and we began the drive to wherever they were taking.

Eventually, the ambulance stopped. The doors to the ambulance opened and they let me out. They told me that I would have to go sign myself in. I got out of the ambulance and walked towards the entrance of the rehab. When I went in, I talked to the receptionist. She told me to wait and that someone would come talk to me.

Eventually, that person came and got me. She took me into her office and explained that I was accepted into the detox, but not the rehab. This meant that I had three days there to detox and then would be released. She asked where I planned on going after and I told her I would have to go to a recovery house as I had no other options.

They attempted to give me methadone to detox me, but I refused it because I knew I needed a clean urine to get into a recovery house. I had never turned down drugs before and it was strange to say no to free drugs, but I knew I had to. They gave me another non-narcotic medication to help with the withdrawal. It made me drowsy, so I spent the majority of my time in the rehab sleeping. I didn't attend any of the groups. All I did was sleep.

The second day that I was there, they told me that I needed to set up a recovery house for me to go to when I was released. They gave me a list of recovery houses and a phone. The first one that I called answered. I explained my situation through tears and they told me they had a bed. I would be able to go there when I was released.

I was relieved because I had dug myself out of this hole. I had gotten high and fucked everything up, but I got through it. Now, I would be going back to another recovery house. This time, there would be no fucking up. I had no option except to stay sober. Sobriety was my only option. Well, the alternative was to be homeless and I didn't want that.

I slept through the rest of my stay at the detox. The day I was released, they loaded me into a van. The recovery house I was going to was in Levittown again. I was going right back to the place I had just left.

When I got to the house, I was greeted by the house manager yet again. I told them my situation and we completed the paperwork quickly because I had just gone through this process about two weeks ago.

My mindset was completely fucked up. I was completely physically and emotionally broken. When I went into the rehab a few months ago, I was one hundred and forty pounds. I now weight one hundred and eighty-five pounds. So, you can imagine how unhealthy I looked. My emotions were all over the place as well. I had found myself back in a recovery house with nowhere else to go.

I decided that I would have to give being sober a chance. There was no other option for me.

I would follow the house rules and attempt to recover from addiction. I would have to get a job and learn how to live on my own. It was time for me to grow up and become an active member of society.

This was not an easy task for me. All I had known for the last four years was getting high and everything that is involved with using. I had no idea on how to live on my own and be a normal person. It was not going to be an easy journey, but it was a journey that I had to take.

So, I started following the rules exactly how they were laid out. I started going to meetings and did the things that I had to do to stay sober. I got a job pretty quickly because I had put applications in when I was in the last house and the companies were starting to get back to me. I ended up taking a job at Wawa. It was only about thirty hours a week, but I would be making enough money to pay for what I needed.

The only bills I had to pay were my rent and phone bill. Therefore, my expenses were pretty low and I could get by only working thirty hours a week. It wasn't the best job or highest paying, but it would keep me busy.

Over the next few months, I began to learn how to live my life without drugs. I showed up to work and went to meetings. That was pretty much my entire life. The rest of the time was spent hanging out with guys from the house I lived in. We were all pretty close in age and everyone got along pretty well.

I no longer considered using heroin as an option in my life. I had gone long enough to know that staying sober was the only option for me. Yet, I still did think about heroin. I just didn't think about using it.

About three months in to my sobriety, I decided that I was going to join the Army. It was something I had always wanted to do, but couldn't because I was doing drugs. Now that I was sober, I thought that this was the best career choice for me. I didn't want to go to college, so it seemed that joining the Army was the best route to take.

I went into an Army recruitment center and began the process of signing up. I told them that I was a recovering addict and they told me not to mention that on the paperwork. They said as long as I didn't tell anyone else, no one would ever find out.

Once I was done signing up, they had me go take the ASFAB, which is a test to determine what jobs you are eligible for in the Army. I ended up scoring almost perfectly on the test, which allowed me to choose from a long list of jobs that I wanted. The job that I chose was an intelligence analyst. The reason that I chose it was because when I completed my four years in the Army, I would be able to go back to civilian life to a job that would pay well.

The only problem with this job was that I would need to get a top-secret clearance. That meant that an Army investigator would be digging into my life to see if there was any reason that I wouldn't receive the clearance.

The first time that I met with the investigator, I told him everything. I told him I was a recovering addict and that he would find that out when looking into my past. He wondered why that was not on my paperwork and I told him that the recruiters told me to lie about it. He was going to see what he could do about the situation, but he could make no promises.

I was scheduled to leave for boot camp in May. I had a few more months to spend in the recovery house before I would start my career in the military. I was excited to finally be moving my life in the right direction.

My parents decided to book a vacation for us before I left for boot camp. I was going to leave the recovery house two weeks before boot camp and we were going to go to Florida for a few days. The next week I would spend at my parent's house before leaving for boot camp.

The next few months went by quickly and before I knew it, it was time to leave the recovery house. It was a bitter sweet moment because this house had taught me how to live a sober life and provided me with the opportunity to join the Army. I was also leaving all the friends that I had made while I was there, but I was ready to take the next step in life.

My parents picked me up from the house and we were heading straight to the airport to leave for Florida. I said my goodbyes to everyone and loaded my things into my parent's car. I was excited to have some downtime with my parents before I left for boot camp.

When I left that house, I had no intention of using drugs ever again. All I wanted to do was to have a good vacation and then start my military career. If you would have told me when I left the house that I would relapse within twenty-four hours, I would not have believed you. Yet, that was exactly what was going to happen. Something was going to change in my mind and I was going to go back to drugs.

When we arrived in Florida and got to the hotel, something in my mind changed. I realized I had two weeks before I was going to go to boot camp and I wanted to get high before I left. All of a sudden, the obsession to get high was back in my mind and that's what I was going to do. I was going to get high in Florida.

I knew that finding heroin in Florida might not be that easy, but finding Percocet would be rather easy. Florida had a huge prescription pill problem back then and finding someone who had Percocet would be easier than finding heroin.

We didn't arrive at our hotel until night time. We had no plans for the next day and I decided that's when I would go find Percocet. I went to sleep that night and woke up excited the next day because I was going to get high. I didn't care that I was once again going to throw away six months of sobriety. My only care was getting high.

This time was different because I wasn't getting high because of Anna. I was getting high because I wanted to get high. I realized that maybe Anna was only a justification to get high. Her actions gave me an excuse to go back to drugs and

I used it every time. I think the reason I blamed her so much was because it made me feel better about getting high. I had someone who I could put the blame on for my actions. When in reality, I was the one who was getting high. She wasn't shoving a needle in my arm, I was. She was just an excuse that I used.

I told my parents that I was going for a walk. They were going to get lunch and we were going to meet back at the hotel room in a few hours. This gave me some time to go find something to get high on. I was searching for Percocet, but I would do any opiate that I could find.

Our hotel was right on the beach, there was a lot of shops that lined the beach area. I started walking by all the shops looking for someone that might have drugs. I saw a few kids skateboarding. They were about my age and I decided to approach them.

"Hey man."

"Do I know you?"

"Na, I'm just here on vacation. I'm trying to find Percocet."

He laughed. "You actually caught me at the perfect time, I'm about to go pick some up."

"What a coincidence."

The thing about being a drug addict is that for some reason we are able to spot other people like us. If you put me anywhere in the world, I guarantee I could find drugs within an hour. It's just a skill that we develop. I had found Percocet in Florida within fifteen minutes of my search beginning.

"You're not a cop, are you?"

"Na, I'm just trying to get high man."

"How many do you want? I got to let the guy know that we're picking up from."

"How much are they?"

"There thirty milligrams and it's a dollar a milligram."

That was a high price, but I didn't really care. I didn't know how long it would take to find someone else that could get them. So, I agreed to that price. I assumed he was up charging me so that he could make a couple bucks on the deal.

"That's cool. I'll take three. Where do we have to go to get them?"

"It's about fifteen minutes away. You can come with us."

He yelled over to his girlfriend to let her know it was time to go. He led us over to his car and the three of us hopped in. We chatted throughout the car ride. I told them pretty much my entire story. I wanted to ensure them that I wasn't a cop. By the time I was done, they knew I wasn't a cop.

We pulled up to a house. The kid that was driving turned around. "I need the money from you. I'm going to go in to grab them and be right back. She will stay here with you."

I handed him ninety dollars and he got out of the car. We both waited for him to come back. It was about five minutes before he came back out of the house. He got in the car and immediately handed me three pills. I checked to make sure they had the correct markings on them. They were real.

I put them in my cigarette pack to save them for later.

The girl asked me, "You're not going to do any now?"

"No, I want to wait to get back to the hotel."

"Okay."

The two of them proceeded to break down their pills and snort them. I just watched as both of them got high. I wasn't anxious to get high. I knew I would be high soon enough. I wanted to wait to get back to the room so that I could do my drugs in peace. I didn't like doing drugs with other people. I knew that I would be more comfortable doing mine at the hotel.

They dropped me off at my hotel and I went up to the room. I went straight into the bathroom. I crushed up half of one of the pills. I knew that half of one would be enough to get me high. I hadn't done any drugs in the last six months, so half a pill would suffice. I needed to save the rest for the rest of the trip. We were only there for two more days, so I had enough to last the whole trip.

I stared at the line of Percocet that I had cut up on the bathroom sink. I knew that I was about to relapse again. I wondered how my mindset had changed so quickly. What had happened? How did I end up doing drugs yet again?

I didn't have an answer. So, I did the only thing I knew how to do. I snorted that line and tasted the drugs as they went down my nasal passage. There was no remorse about getting high. I had come to terms with the fact that I was a drug addict. This was how my life was going to go.

I spent the rest of the vacation getting high and hanging out with my parents. They had no idea that I had relapsed. They were never good at noticing the signs of me getting high. That's part of the reason that I was always able to get away with it.

When we returned home, I immediately got heroin. I had nine days left before I left for boot camp. I was going to get high for five of those days and the next four I would clean out my system. I couldn't show up to boot camp with a hot urine.

I ran out of heroin on the last day that I wanted to get high. I had to go pick up more. I asked one of my friends to get it for me because I knew he was going down the city to get more. We planned to meet up that night so that I could pick it up from him.

That night, he called me on his way back. He had picked up the heroin and was going to be home in about thirty minutes. I had Jake come pick me up so that I could go get the heroin.

When we got to my friend's house, he wasn't answering his phone. We didn't know what to do. We waited for about thirty minutes. We kept calling his phone with no answer. We figured that he had shot some heroin and nodded out. We decided to just go home. I ended up buying coke from Jake, so that I had something to get high on. I never really liked coke, but it was all I could get.

That night, I shot all of the coke I bought. I spent the whole night doing shot after shot of coke. It turns out that my last high ever would be a cocaine high. I would never use again after that night. It's weird that my last high wasn't heroin, but it doesn't really matter.

The next day I woke up to a call from my friend Jake.

"What's up?"

"Connor's dead."

Connor was who we went to meet up with to get the heroin.

"What happened?"

"He overdosed last night. If we would have knocked on his door, we probably would have saved his life."

"Dude, we thought he nodded out."

"I know, but it still hurts knowing we were only a hundred yards away."

"There's nothing we can do now. Don't beat yourself up over it."

"I know. I got to go man. I'll talk to you later."

I had just lost another friend to heroin. Jake and I were literally at his house when he had overdosed. I had told Jake not to beat himself up, but I was beating myself up. I know that if we just would have knocked on his door, he would have been found. They probably would have been able to revive him and he would still be alive.

The other scary part was that if we had gotten there a little earlier, I would have shot the heroin that killed him. I very well could have been the one that overdosed instead. Once again, my life was spared for some reason.

The next few days I spent doing absolutely nothing. I couldn't do drugs because I needed clean urine. There was nothing for me to do at the house. I spent the days just watching movies. I was enjoying the last few days of relaxation before going to boot camp.

The day finally came to leave for boot camp. My recruiter was going to pick me up and take me to the hotel. I would spend the night at the hotel and leave from there to go to boot camp.

My recruiter picked me up and dropped me off at the hotel. I checked in and had a dinner that was provided by the hotel for all the Army recruits. I went to my room afterwards and watched a movie until I fell asleep.

I woke up the next morning at five. I went down and got breakfast. Just before we were going to board the bus, I heard my name called. It was the Army investigator. He was walking over to me.

"Dan, I need you to come with me."

"Okay."

I followed him. He walked over to a part of the lobby where no one was.

"I have bad news for you."

"What's that?"

"Your top-secret clearance was denied."

"Why?"

"It was denied because of your trips to drug rehab. If your recruiters had you fill out the correct paperwork, there would have been no issues. Yet, since they instructed you to lie, it had been denied. You will be able to go through the process again in six months if you would like."

"So, what happens now?"

"I called your recruiter, they are coming to pick you up and take you home."

"Thank you."

I was pissed. The only reason I had lied was because I was told to do so. Now, I had to go home. I didn't know what would happen when I got home. I don't think that my parents wanted me to stay there. My plan had been ruined. I was once again completely lost.

Chapter 24

After Connor died, I knew I had to get sober. I believed it was a wakeup call for me. I very easily could have been Connor. I could have died at any point throughout my addiction. I had no regard for how precious my life was. I didn't care. All I cared about was getting high. I was now at a point where I either had to get sober or I knew I was going to die. I didn't want to live life without drugs, but I knew I couldn't live life with drugs either.

I called my parents and told them what had happened. They told me that I needed to go back to the recovery house. They didn't want me living with them. I knew that was what was going to happen. It was the right decision. They had no idea I had relapsed, but I needed to go back to the recovery house. It was the only way I was ever going to figure out how to live a sober life.

My parents drove me back to the recovery house that I had left two weeks earlier. My life had changed dramatically in those two weeks. I had relapsed, not been allowed to go to boot camp and I had another friend die due to addiction. I was coming back to the recovery house with my head hung even lower than the first time I showed up.

When I got back, one of my friends was there waiting to talk to me. His name was Frank and he is a big part of the reason that I stayed sober. When I got to the house, he brought be outside. We began talking about why I relapsed and what I planned to do different this time.

I told him, "I honestly don't want to be sober, but I don't want to get high anymore. I really don't want to be here, but I know I need to be. I really want to go get high."

"Well, how about you give it six months. In six months, if things don't get better, go get high. The drugs will always be there. They're not going anywhere. So, if you still want to get high in six months, do it. For now, give being sober a real chance. My guess is that in six months you won't want to get high. Your life will improve and you will want to stay sober."

"Okay."

"Promise me that you will give it six months."

"I promise."

That was the beginning of my journey to sobriety. For the first three months, I really wanted to die. I didn't want to live anymore if I couldn't use drugs. Yet, I had made Frank a promise that I intended to uphold.

I began to do the things that I had to do to stay sober. I went to Alcoholics Anonymous meetings and I got a sponsor. A sponsor is someone that guides you through the Twelve Steps that are supposed to help you stay sober. I began going through the steps with my sponsor. I was beginning to deal with the fact that I would be a recovering addict for the rest of my life.

The steps are designed to make you realize that you are a drug addict and that you are completely powerless over all mind-altering substances. I had no problem accepting that. I had known I was a drug addict for a long time. I had come to terms with that fact years ago.

The steps are also designed to find a higher power and clear the wreckage of your past. I was more than happy to clear the wreckage of my past, but I always struggled with the higher power aspect. I didn't believe in god and most people use god as their higher power. For me, I decided that Ava would be my higher power.

I got a job at cabinet factory that was full time and went back to my job at Wawa part time. I was now working more than sixty hours a week. Between work and meetings, my schedule was completely full. I didn't really have any time to do anything else. That was exactly what I needed.

I knew that I needed to make progress in my life in order to want to stay sober. I decided that I would go to college so that I could eventually get a good job. I signed up for community college and I was scheduled to start in the fall. I planned to work both jobs until school started. Then, I would only work part time at Wawa so that I could focus on school.

Shortly after starting college, I started my own business. The business that I started was a moving company. At first, I worked at Wawa while running the business as well. Once the business picked up, I quit Wawa so that I could run the business full time.

These small steps were what helped me to get sober. I began to build a life for myself that I didn't want to lose. I knew that if I relapsed that I would lose everything that I had worked for. Therefore, when I was six months sober, I decided that I wanted to stay sober for the rest of my life. It wouldn't be an easy process, but I knew it was the only life that I wanted.

I now have six years of sobriety. I graduated college with a degree in accounting. My business still exists. In fact, I handed off to my first employee. He now runs the company so that I can focus on other ventures. I am currently working on a start-up company.

For now, this is the end of the story. I laid out my whole journey through hell for you. I did make it through to the other side. I survived all that bullshit in order to live the life that I live today. Without all of my experiences, I don't believe I would where I am today.

Today, I like the person that I am. Life isn't perfect, it never is. Yet, today I get through everything without using drugs. I have found a better way of life and I intend to continue down that path.

Sure, there will be bumps along the way, but as long as I don't pick up a drink or a drug, I will make it through.

Made in the USA
Columbia, SC
19 March 2020